BULLYING

in Canada

FAYE MISHNA AND MELISSA VAN WERT

ISSUES IN CANADA

OXFORD
UNIVERSITY PRESS

OXFORD
UNIVERSITY PRESS

Oxford University Press is a department of the University of Oxford.
It furthers the University's objective of excellence in research, scholarship,
and education by publishing worldwide. Oxford is a registered trade mark of
Oxford University Press in the UK and in certain other countries.

Published in Canada by
Oxford University Press
8 Sampson Mews, Suite 204,
Don Mills, Ontario M3C 0H5 Canada

www.oupcanada.com

Library and Archives Canada Cataloguing in Publication

Mishna, Faye, author
Bullying in Canada / Faye Mishna and Melissa Van Wert.

(Issues in Canada)
Includes bibliographical references and index.
ISBN 978-0-19-900304-4 (pbk.)

1. Bullying—Canada. I. Wert, Melissa van, author
II. Title. III. Series: Issues in Canada

BF637.B85M58 2014   302.34'3   C2014-904499-2

Cover image: ClarkandCompany/iStockphoto

Oxford University Press is committed to our environment.
Wherever possible, our books are printed on paper which comes from
responsible sources.

Printed and bound in Canada

1 2 3 4—18 17 16 15

Contents

Acknowledgements

We would like to thank Jennifer Millson and Tyler Cohen for their contribution to Chapters 2 and 3. We would also like to thank Cindy Blackstock for her contribution to Chapter 3.

This work draws on our previous research. For full information about these sources, see the works listed under Mishna in the reference list.

Chapter 1

Defining and Determining the Frequency and Effects of Bullying

Introduction

Bullying is widespread, and too often results in long-term developmental or other problems for individuals. As with many social issues, bullying is a multi-faceted, complex problem. The best ways to define, prevent, and address it are matters of ongoing debate. In spite of the complexities, however, adults have a duty to intervene: protection from abuse is a fundamental human right.[1] Canada is one of the countries that have ratified the United Nations Convention on the Rights of the Child. This convention states that children everywhere have the right to survive and to develop to the fullest, as well as to be protected from harm, abuse, and exploitation (UNICEF 2013b). The bullying of young people is a serious and pervasive worldwide phenomenon that threatens these core values and compromises healthy development.

A common schoolyard experience that many of us can remember from our own childhoods, bullying has been a normalized and often unspoken part of growing up (Tutty et al. 2005). In fact, it is considered "the most prevalent form of low-level violence in schools today" (Whitted & Dupper 2005, 167).[2] It has been tolerated in Western society, even touted as an experience that builds character. Although this view persists—and may in fact even be perpetuated by the sheer pervasiveness of bullying—there is growing recognition that it is a serious public health issue.

Bullying as a phenomenon was first studied in Sweden in the late 1960s and 1970s. Interest intensified after the 1982 suicides of three boys who were associated with bullying victimization. Dan Olweus is considered to be the first scholar to conduct research on bullying, carrying out studies in both Norway and Sweden in the early 1980s. Olweus developed and evaluated an anti-bullying program, launched by the Norwegian Ministry of Education, which targeted the whole school, the classroom, and individual students.[3] Research interest and anti-bullying programs have since grown internationally, involving a variety of methodologies to collect and examine data. Most studies employ a survey design; fewer studies use qualitative methods.

In recent years we have seen the emergence of cyberbullying, with unique implications for prevention and intervention. Children and youth now develop within the context of a "cyber world," wherein information and communication technologies serve as a primary medium through which to relate to peers, friends, and family. While it is no surprise that cyberbullying has developed in the context of the new cyber world, concern about this recent phenomenon has been growing in the wake of several high-profile cases of suicide in which cyberbullying was considered a contributing factor. Most recently, recall the tragic deaths of Amanda Todd and Rehtaeh Parsons, both sad and complex cases of suicides that drew considerable media attention. As suicide is multi-determined, it is unlikely that bullying was the sole cause of these tragedies, although the deaths of these teenage girls sparked intense debate and concern about both traditional bullying and cyberbullying. Developing effective policies and practices is proving difficult, but efforts are underway in Canada and internationally. In Chapter 2 of this book, we review the latest research on cyberbullying and discuss efforts to put an end to it in Canada and abroad.[4]

Both "traditional" face-to-face bullying and cyberbullying can be motivated by bias. Any type of bullying that is motivated by intolerance or hatred toward others based on actual or perceived membership in a particular group, such as gender, race, religion, sexual orientation, ability, or socio-economic status, is known as "bias-based bullying" (Greene 2006; Stein 2003). This harmful form of bullying is the subject of Chapter 3. It takes place frequently, and those who belong to marginalized groups or minority groups are more vulnerable. A recent Canadian survey found that 70 percent of high school students reported hearing homophobic expressions like "that's so gay" every day in school, and many trans and sexual minority youth reported experiencing verbal, physical, and sexual harassment (Taylor et al. 2011). The majority of both heterosexual and sexual minority youth found homophobic comments upsetting, according to the study. American research confirms the harmful impact of bias-based harassment, linking it to poor mental health and substance use (Russell et al. 2012).

Following the first three chapters of this book, which consider the various types and forms of bullying, we discuss two particular relationships in which any type or form can occur: friendships and sibling relationships. This may come as a surprise to some, as many people do not think about bullying occurring in such relationships. It can be challenging to distinguish between mutual conflict among friends or siblings and situations of bullying. Once identified, bullying in these relationships must be carefully assessed in order to determine the best response. We discuss these and other issues in more detail in Chapter 4.

Bullying is a common childhood experience, and its complexity is often overlooked. In Chapter 5, we present and analyze several case examples to illustrate the complex scenarios that occur among children and adolescents. It is critically important to understand these complexities in order to develop appropriate strategies to prevent and end bullying situations. In the sixth and final chapter, current anti-bullying initiatives are reviewed along with evidence for their effectiveness.

Definition

Much effort has gone toward developing a clear and comprehensive definition, but a lack of consensus remains. Furthermore, the technical definitions of bullying used by experts and researchers rarely align with the definition used by children, adolescents, parents, and educators in day-to-day life. Research shows that young people seldom include the same criteria in their definitions of bullying as researchers do, although both groups—young people and researchers alike—do, by and large, agree on some features. In a recent publication (Mishna 2012), the features on which most agree were described in detail; a summary will be presented here.

Bullying is a form of aggression. It can be direct or indirect and includes physical, verbal, psychological, or relational acts. It is typically intentional and always occurs in the context of a relationship. It also generally involves a power imbalance, and the aggressive behaviour is repeated over time.[5]

It is worth looking at this definition in a little more detail. First, as a form of aggression, bullying can damage a young person's sense of self and peer relationships. There are distinctions between direct and indirect forms of aggression, although it is worth noting that children and youth who use either form share similar risk factors.[6]

Direct aggression can be physical or verbal: hitting, pushing, kicking, and making verbal threats or putdowns. Examples include pushing a peer into his or her locker, threatening a trembling sibling by saying, "You'd better run," or posting a status update on a social networking site in which an acquaintance is called a derogatory name in all-capital letters. It is generally easier for adults to detect direct aggression because it is overt and can be easily observed. *Indirect aggression,* sometimes described as "meanness," can involve exclusion, gossip, and ridicule. The goal is often to manipulate social networks. Several forms of indirect aggression have been described in the bullying literature, including relational, reputational, and social or psychological aggression. Although there is overlap, we consider each of these separately below.

Relational aggression involves manipulating relationships in order to cause harm. It may include breaking confidences, talking just loud enough or within earshot so that the targeted peer hears, or behaviour such as excluding or ignoring someone. *Reputational aggression* is often used to heighten one's position on the social hierarchy, and may include spreading rumours, gossiping, and manipulating friendships. As with other forms of indirect aggression, it is challenging for adults to detect *social aggression,* which can include ridicule, intimidation, and group rejection. *Psychological bullying* can represent a direct attack on a young person's sense of self-worth, as it often involves mocking an individual on the basis of personal characteristics, such as appearance, personality, race, gender, or family. Other examples include extending an invitation to a peer and then leaving him stranded or "stood up," calling a peer's house in the middle of the night to anonymously say that everyone at school hates her, and switching tables or saying the seat is "taken" to avoid sitting with a peer as soon as she sits down nearby at lunch. Even nonverbal and subtle forms of psychological bullying can be powerful and extremely upsetting. One child may give another a certain "look" or "face" every time she tries to speak up in class. Another child may roll his eyes at a peer whenever it is his turn to bat in baseball at recess. These more subtle forms of aggression are very difficult to detect even when teachers and other adults are present.[7]

Unfortunately, some of the most common and hurtful forms of aggression are often not considered to be bullying. One study found that pre-service teachers in Ontario were less likely to think of relational, homophobic, and cyberbullying as serious and problematic compared to physical forms of bullying (Craig, Bell, & Leschied 2011). There is an ingrained perception that certain common and subtle aggressive behaviours are "minor" or "harmless"—for example, everyday language such as "that's so gay" or "you're such a fag." A consequence of this is that the damage inflicted by certain types of bullying can be overlooked. If teachers regard indirect bullying as less detrimental, they may be less likely to intervene in situations of indirect aggression and to have less empathy for victimized children. Indeed, the vast majority of teachers ignore subtle forms of aggression, hoping or thinking the students will resolve the issue on their own.[8] Yet, if adults do not respond, "what the children learn from the adults' handling of bullying incidents must be more frightening to them than the individual bullying incidents" (Clarke & Kiselica 1997, 316). In contrast, there are other situations in which an adult may consider an incident to be bullying whereas a child may not. Such situations underscore the need for adults to intervene in a manner that is sensitive but protective.[9]

In a study conducted in Ontario with our colleagues,[10] we interviewed students in grades four and five who self-identified as victimized, as well as their parents, teachers, and school administrators. We administered the "Safe School Questionnaire"[11] to 157 students to obtain their self-reports of bullying behaviour in school. Parents, teachers, and school administrators talked about situations in which the child respondents were involved. Most of the participants included both direct and indirect forms of aggression in their definitions. We found, however, that adults and children alike often "normalized" indirect bullying; this may cause them to unwittingly minimize or overlook non-physical aggression. The minimization of indirect bullying corresponds with wider international literature on the subject. In fact, many of the participants in our study appeared to use a hierarchy to categorize bullying behaviours, whereby direct forms were considered more serious than indirect forms. One girl, for instance, included exclusion and gossip in her definition of bullying, but later stated that this type of behaviour was "less serious."

Teachers in the study interpreted incidents in various ways, which influenced whether they viewed the incident as "normal" or problematic and also influenced whether they responded. One teacher, for example, was very surprised that a particular student identified himself as being bullied, because he had friends and appeared to be well-liked. This particular teacher also believed that physical behaviours were more serious than verbal or indirect forms. When this boy had complained about being bullied to this teacher, she did not "take him seriously." Her understanding of bullying clearly limited her ability to respond in some situations.

Several teachers who appeared to understand the significance of indirect bullying did not know how to respond when they encountered it. For example, one teacher described an incident in which a boy pulled down a girl's pants, which was witnessed by other girls who then told the teacher the girl had pulled down her own pants. After the boy finally admitted what he had done, the teacher responded firmly by sending him to the office, where he was suspended. The teacher did not respond, however, to the girls who had lied about the incident. She decided not to because she was afraid that would make the situation worse. By not responding, this teacher missed an opportunity to address indirect bullying and also failed to send a message to students that it can be just as harmful as direct forms.

A major barrier that prevents teachers from responding to bullying situations is a lack of time. Even if teachers recognize the harm associated with all forms of bullying, and are aware of how to respond, they need to have the time and resources to enable them to identify problematic situations and intervene effectively. Many of the teachers who participated in our study told us that dealing with bullying incidents in addition to their other responsibilities was overwhelming, particularly because these incidents seemed to go on "all day every day" and because it was sometimes challenging to distinguish "normal" conflict from bullying, thus making it difficult to know how to respond.

There is some consensus that intent to cause harm to an individual is an integral part of the definition of bullying. In most cases, the concept of aggression implies intent to inflict injury or discomfort on another person. That injury or discomfort can be mental, emotional, or physical. But what about situations in which a child feels bullied while the child who carried out the bullying does not appear to have the intention to hurt? Some think that the feelings of the victimized child should be prioritized, regardless of the perpetrator's intentions. It is no surprise, however, that it is difficult to ascertain a child's intentions at any given moment.

Determining the intentions of a young person usually comes after an analysis of the *context* of an incident. Should the young person have known or understood that the behaviour would be experienced as distressing by the targeted person? If so, it is usually safe to assume that the aggression was intentional. There may be situations in which a young person *should* have known, but *did not* know that his or her behaviour could cause harm. In these cases, it is important to seriously consider the reasons for a young person's lack of awareness, as this may provide crucial information to help prevent bullying in the future. Take, for instance, a situation in which a teenage boy tells a crude joke to a group of peers about a gay couple. A girl in the group may feel quite hurt by the joke, perhaps because she has parents or other relatives who are gay, or perhaps because she is questioning her own sexual identity. The joke teller may not have known this, and may not have intended for anyone to be hurt by the joke. This does not mean, however, that the girl's distress is not important or valid, nor does it mean that the boy's joke is acceptable. Clearly, it is important to consider whether this boy is accepting of sexual minorities like gay and lesbian people, and whether he is aware of the discrimination they face in our society. Upon learning about some of these issues, he may be more sensitive and more aware of the potential harm that could come from a "joke." The way awareness is taught or promoted must take into consideration the developmental stage of the young person in question.

Intention is even more difficult to understand in situations of cyberbullying. Consider the following situation. A teenage girl covertly takes a photo on her cellphone of an overweight classmate in the school locker room and emails it to her best friend, with the subject line, "Ew!" Her best friend then uploads the photo to a web group on a social networking site with a degrading comment regarding weight. Most students at the school have access to the site. The original sender only intended for her best friend to see the image, and she feels terrible upon learning about its broader distribution. What is her role in this incident of cyberbullying? She should have recognized the potential for the image to be widely distributed, even though she did not actually distribute it. Most of all, she should have recognized that clandestinely taking a photo of someone in a private space is wrong, and that sending a private image to someone without the consent of the person represented in that image is wrong. In this example, even though the original sender did not intend to bully the girl in the locker room, she clearly requires help in understanding issues related to indirect aggression, privacy, "netiquette," and cyberbullying.[12]

There has been a significant shift in the bullying field over the past several years, with researchers placing greater emphasis on bullying as a relationship problem rather than a problem located within a specific aggressive child or a particularly vulnerable victim. One recent definition, put forth by Wendy Craig and Debra Pepler, leading bullying experts in Canada, describes bullying as a "destructive relationship problem," in which "children who bully are learning to use power and aggression to control and distress others; children who are victimized become increasingly powerless and unable to defend themselves from this peer abuse" (Craig & Pepler 2007, 86). Leaders in promoting this concept of bullying, Craig and Pepler argue that children require help from adults to learn how to connect with others respectfully in positive and healthy ways. Furthermore, they point out that healthy development among children and youth is truly dependent on healthy relationships. When we think about bullying as a relationship problem, we can more easily avoid blaming the perpetrator—or worse, the victim. We can also more easily recognize the connection between bullying and overall child and youth well-being.

An important element of the definition is an imbalance of power. Children who bully typically have more power than those they victimize. Again, we come to the problem of finding a way to define an interpersonal phenomenon that is open to interpretation: how do we define power imbalance? Power dynamics may be very clear in some situations, but not in others. Relatively objective factors, such as physical strength or popularity, might distinguish who holds more power in some bullying situations. In others, however, power may be derived through less obvious means such as structural or systemic factors (e.g., race, culture, sexual identity, disability status) or knowledge of another's vulnerabilities (e.g., learning problem, family background).

In the study referred to above, the children discussed imbalances of power in bullying situations: "older kids think they can overpower the little ones," and "it's the kids' fault because they think that they're powerful." Parents and teachers also noted the issue of power differences. A parent talked about "one child trying to exert their power towards another child to intimidate." A teacher described a child who bullies as "trying to get some kind of power or control over that person," and a principal described bullying as an individual "putting another in a position where they are intimidated or feel they need to do something they are not comfortable with." Although it was clear to most participants that power dynamics influence bullying situations, most adults had a difficult time actually detecting when an imbalance existed. According to one teacher, "It can be very hard to decide whether it really is a bullying situation, whether it's one up, one down, or 50-50." It is important to keep in mind that children and youth rarely fit readily into one category, such as "the bully" or "the victim." Given the many difficulties in making an assessment, it may be best to focus on the power imbalance as it is perceived by the targeted person.[13]

Can a situation be considered bullying if it only happens once? Some researchers would say "no." Repetition is often considered key in defining bullying. If a negative behaviour is repetitive, we can be more certain that the behaviour is intentional, which may make detecting bullying somewhat easier. Some argue, however, that focusing on repetition can be limiting, as under some circumstances a single serious instance might be an act of bullying.[14]

What defines repetition? It may imply that actual incidents of bullying are repeated over time; it may also refer to the fear of future victimization, which can be triggered by even one incident. The harmful consequences of repetitive bullying, regardless of the severity of a particular incident, are well documented—as is the fear of future incidents, which can intensify a child's distress.[15] Indeed, the dread of future occurrences and stress were apparent in the children who participated in our study. Based on these findings, it is reasonable to conclude that repetition is an important aspect of the bullying dynamic, either in light of actual repetition or in causing fear and anxiety.

Gender Differences

Boys tend to use direct bullying, while girls are prone to use more indirect forms. American researchers Nicki Crick and Jennifer Grotpeter, in their seminal work on gender and bullying, proposed that children enact aggression in ways that best damage the goals valued by their gender peer groups. For boys, physical dominance and appearing "tough" or "macho" are key concerns in the peer group context. Girls, on the other hand, tend to be more concerned with establishing close, intimate relationships. These researchers hypothesized that aggression among boys and girls would differ based on the primary social concerns for each gender, and their study provided support for this hypothesis. Interestingly, the percentage of girls identified as aggressive was almost equal to the percentage of boys identified as such, although girls primarily used relational aggression. A later study, conducted by researchers Sara Goldstein and Marie Tisak, found similar levels of relational aggression across adolescent girls and boys, although their self-reported beliefs about the outcomes of this type of behaviour varied. Young women tended to associate more negative consequences with relational aggression compared to young men.

In a qualitative study that focused on what happens when girls are aggressive toward others, researchers Laurence Owens and colleagues found that talking or "bitching" (Owens, Shute, & Slee 2000, 72) about others was the most predominant form of aggression among girls. Other common forms of relational aggression included spreading rumours, breaking confidences, using code names to talk about others, and criticizing others' clothes, appearance, or personality. The girls felt these behaviours were "second nature," as if they couldn't help themselves or acting this way was out of their control. Other kinds of interpersonal conduct, clearly more deliberate, included exclusionary behaviours, such as ignoring friends or purposely leaving certain peers out of activities for long periods of time. The participants talked about the direct aggression displayed by girls as well, such as overt put-downs, slaps, elbowing, and tripping. When explaining why girls engage in indirect aggression, some participants said it was for attention or to be included, and others said it was simply something to do to alleviate boredom. Referring to the structure of the playground, the researchers noted that boys were more active at lunch and other break times, participating in sports or other activities, whereas girls tended to congregate and talk in small groups at these times. With fewer activities in which to engage during break, perhaps girls resorted to indirect aggression as a means of generating excitement. Meanwhile, boys may have been engaging in physical forms of aggression on the football field or baseball diamond. It is not surprising that girls and boys engage in different forms of aggression, as the two groups are socialized much differently from the moment they are born.

Canadian researchers Dawn Currie, Deirdre Kelly, and Shauna Pomerantz considered girls' relational aggression from a feminist perspective, specifically examining the concept of "meanness." In interviews with 28 girls, these researchers found that meanness encompassed behaviours such as ridicule, name calling, backstabbing, gossip, as well as the silent treatment, and was used by girls to harm the social presence of other girls as well as to regulate membership in friendship cliques. The participating girls told researchers that although meanness was often associated with popularity and power, popular girls were actually often not well-liked. The so-called popular girls were described as having to look perfect to get attention from boys and maintain their status, without exuding too much sex appeal. Despite the many negative descriptions of popular girls, the participants in the study aspired to be part of the popular girl crowd.

The reasons girls engage in relational bullying may be deeply connected to larger issues of gender inequality in our society. With the intense pressure on girls to reach an impossible and antiquated feminine ideal, young women are often pressured to be pretty but not too self-absorbed, attractive to boys but not too sexually forward, included in the peer group but not a social climber, assertive but not masculine—the list goes on. Feeling inadequate and unable to achieve these problematic ideals, girls may lash out at one another as a way of feeling more empowered while also punishing other girls who do not reach these ideals.

It is only within the past 20 years that researchers, educators, and policy makers have paid attention to aggression among girls. In that time, a narrative has developed about the indirect aggression that girls perpetrate. This narrative of "mean" or "bitchy" girls who can ruin the lives of their victims sometimes veers out of control. It is important to remember that both indirect and direct forms of aggression are harmful, and that boys as well as girls engage in each form. While there are gendered patterns in aggressive behaviours, it is imperative to keep in mind that both indirect and direct bullying situations are problematic and consequential.[16]

Prevalence

Large-scale surveys on the prevalence of bullying in schools have been conducted in countries throughout the world, including Australia, Brazil, Canada, England, India, Ireland, Italy, Japan, Korea, Nicaragua, Norway, Sweden, Turkey, and the United States.[17]

Research in over 40 countries involving more than 200,000 adolescents has revealed that approximately 11 percent of participants reported perpetrating bullying, 13 percent reported being targeted, and 4 percent reported being both a perpetrator and a target. Prevalence estimates for involvement in bullying varied considerably across countries, ranging from 9 percent to 45 percent for boys, and 5 percent to 36 percent for girls. The lowest prevalence estimates were reported in Sweden and the highest in Lithuania (Craig et al. 2009).

Why might prevalence estimates vary so drastically across countries? Certain behaviours may be more acceptable in some countries. In many languages, in fact, there is no equivalent word for the term "bullying." Both of these factors influence the reported prevalence and intervention rates. In addition, each country has a different tradition of bullying research, prevention, and intervention. Scandinavia has a long tradition of bullying research and anti-bullying programming, which may explain the low rates of bullying in Sweden and several other Scandinavian countries. Findings may also vary due to differences in the developmental stage and age of involved youth, as well as the methodologies and research designs used across studies.

Some studies use children's self-reports, whereas others gather the perspectives of teachers or parents, and still others use a peer nomination method to measure bullying. Other studies involve observing children and youth with their peers in order to assess behaviours. Using a self-report method, young people are asked about their experiences with various forms of bullying, usually in a questionnaire format. Even though the responses on these questionnaires are almost always confidential, there is still the potential for young people to withhold the truth about their involvement in bullying due to embarrassment, fears of getting in trouble, or other reasons. Another important consideration is that survey questionnaires vary in quality. Some are too long, and children and youth might not want or be able to pay attention until the end of the questionnaire, instead completing the answers haphazardly. Some are too short and general, and do not accurately capture the range and complexity of bullying experiences.

Teacher and parent reports of bullying can provide a different perspective, perhaps more of an outsider point of view. These reports may be clouded by biases about what a "bully" or "victim" looks like, however. Furthermore, relying on such reports can be problematic as some forms of bullying are difficult for adults to detect, and many young people who are bullied (and, of course, those who bully) do not disclose their involvement.

With a peer nomination method, young people rate their peers on measures related to bullying. This provides rich information and multiple assessments of each child or youth, since each child is rated by each and every one of his or her peers. There remains a chance for bias with this method, however, since young people may not accurately nominate their peers.

Observational methods may involve watching interactions among peers in real time, or instead recording these interactions in some way. Researchers may video or audio record live interactions, or rather may keep a running record of some kind of interaction in the cyber world (e.g., copying all posts from an interactive web game to document cyberbullying). Fewer researchers have attempted using observational methods to capture cyber interactions. Researcher Marion Underwood and her colleagues utilized an innovative method to understand adolescent text messaging. Adolescents were provided with BlackBerry devices with service plans paid for by the researchers, with the devices configured so that the content of all messaging —including text, instant, and email messaging—was saved on a secure server. The exact numbers of messages sent and received could then be counted, and the content of the messages could be coded (Underwood et al. 2012).

A drawback of observational methods is that more subtle forms of bullying might go unnoticed, as the researchers might not have the context to understand a specific situation. Once again, there is room for bias to enter when researchers are recording and analyzing observational data. Further, when the participants are aware they are being observed, the presence of the researcher might inhibit natural behaviour among children, youth, teachers, and others.

Since each method has shortcomings, it is important to gather information on the prevalence and characteristics of bullying involvement using a number of methodologies, including qualitative methods. Whenever assessing the findings of a particular study, it is crucial to critically examine the sample of children, youth, teachers, or parents who participated, as well as the measures used to assess bullying.[18]

The Canadian Context

Canadian researchers report varying prevalence estimates, probably the result of differences in definitions and measures used across studies. According to the Canadian National Longitudinal Survey of Children and Youth, 12 percent of children are bullied at school and 7 percent are bullied on the way to and from school. This is fairly consistent with the findings from a study in Ontario in which 12 percent of students were identified as victims of bullying, 5 percent as perpetrators, and 4 percent as bully-victims—both perpetrators and targets. A smaller study of early adolescents in Western Canada found that 12 percent of students are victimized and 13 percent are perpetrators at least once a week. In a study conducted in one Toronto elementary school, researchers observed children and noted an average of over two bullying episodes per hour in the classroom and over four per hour in the playground. Teachers often were unaware of bullying and peers were usually reluctant to intervene to stop it. Another longitudinal study conducted in Toronto followed over 800 young people from childhood to mid-adolescence. Forty-two percent of these young people said they had never bullied their peers, whereas the majority reported being perpetrators at some point. About 10 percent engaged in high levels of bullying across time and 35 percent engaged in consistently moderate levels. More generally, the Canadian Council on Social Development reported that over half (53 percent) of Canadian youth between the ages of 10 and 15 have at times felt like outsiders at school, and that the number of young Canadians who reported liking school "very much or quite a bit" (Canadian Council on Social Development 2006) decreased from 1998 to 2000.[19]

The Health Behaviour in School-Age Children (HBSC) survey is a cyclical study that collects information about bullying (among other issues) from young people in countries around the world. In the 1993/1994 cycle of the study in Canada, approximately 42 percent of boys and 28 percent of girls reported bullying others occasionally, and 34 percent of boys and 27 percent of girls reported experiencing victimization occasionally. Twelve years later, in the 2005/2006 cycle, the prevalence of occasional bullying among Canadian boys and girls had not decreased; 42 percent of boys and 34 percent of girls reported occasionally bullying others, and 36 percent of boys and 35 percent of girls reported experiencing occasional victimization. This may suggest that between 1993 and 2006, the number of girls perpetrating occasional bullying increased, and more boys and girls experienced bullying victimization in Canada (see Molcho et al. 2009 for these findings). Another interpretation of these findings is that growing awareness in Canada has led to an increase in *disclosures* of bullying. In other words, it may be that more girls and boys are now talking about their experiences, potentially inflating the prevalence estimates; the actual number of children involved in bullying, however, may have decreased. Indeed, there has been an increase in education and knowledge in Canada regarding what constitutes bullying (Mishna, Pepler, et al. 2010). For instance, increased recognition of indirect bullying in the years between 1993 and 2006 may account for the increase in reported prevalence estimates, particularly related to girls' involvement.

One of the biggest challenges to prevention and intervention is that victimized young people will rarely tell adults about their situation. Canadian and international research consistently shows that only a portion of victimized children disclose their experiences. This may be due to the pervasiveness of bullying; if victimization is the norm, young people may not feel disclosure is necessary. A number of Canadian students report that they would tell only when they could no longer "stand" or bear the bullying. These findings reinforce the need for adults to be aware that their child may be involved in bullying and find a way to intervene as early as possible. Children are likely to tell friends about their victimization, but peers may face a dilemma of whether to keep the secret or tell an adult, which may feel like a "betrayal" of the friendship. Not telling is even more problematic among marginalized children and youth, such as sexual minority students, who are more likely to lack supportive family, friends, and teachers. With no safe space and no one to confide in, bullying is particularly dangerous for sexual minority and other marginalized children and youth in Canada.[20]

According to the 2005/2006 HBSC survey, the proportion of students reporting bullying involvement as victim, perpetrator, or both is considerably higher in Canada than it is in many other countries. Canada ranked 21st and 26th out of 40 participating countries on the proportion of boys and girls (respectively) involved in bullying. Several UNICEF reports also rank Canada poorly compared to other rich countries in terms of the quality of family and peer relationships as well as youth behaviours and risks, such as fighting and bullying. Overall, international comparisons suggest that Canada has not been preventing bullying as effectively as other countries around the world.[21]

Canadians are beginning to recognize the importance of bullying prevention and intervention. As a nation, Canada requires and is ready for leadership regarding bullying. We must strike the fine balance between overreacting and underreacting to the problem of bullying: while we should not panic and make assumptions about bullying's negative impact on all of our young people, we must also not ignore or minimize it as a normal part of childhood. The recent parliamentary reviews of bullying and cyberbullying in Canada by the Standing Senate Committee on Human Rights signal progress. Another notable sign of progress in Canada is the development of the Promoting Relationships and Eliminating Violence Network (PREVNet). Established in 2006 with assistance from the federal Networks of Centres of Excellence New Initiative program, PREVNet is a national initiative for promoting healthy relationships and preventing bullying in Canada. PREVNet activities foster interaction, partnership, and networking among researchers and the community. It works with 55 partner organizations across the nation, allowing these organizations to participate in and be informed about the latest research on bullying and the most effective strategies for prevention and intervention. The partners are diverse, ranging from the Boys and Girls Club of Canada to Facebook Canada, the Hospital for Sick Children, Kids Help Phone, and the Canadian National Ballet School. It is the first of its kind in Canada, and it contributes to ending bullying and violence through education, research, training, and policy change. The PREVNet website is an excellent resource for parents, educators, researchers, and anyone else who is interested in learning more about bullying and how to stop it (see www.prevnet.ca).[22]

Effects of Bullying and Associated Issues

Bullying can seriously affect the functioning and well-being of those involved. Children involved as a bully, victim, or both are at risk of developing serious psychosocial and psychiatric problems that may persist into adulthood. Those who are bullied tend to experience problems such as depression and anxiety, and other issues that are focused inward on the self. Clinicians refer to such issues as "internalizing problems." In contrast, children who bully are more likely to display outwardly problematic behaviours such as aggression and antisocial behaviour. These issues have been labelled "externalizing problems" by clinicians.[23]

There is compelling evidence suggesting that many areas of victimized children's lives may be affected, including their academics, their social lives, and their emotional, psychological, and physical health. Young people who are bullied may experience stress-related physical symptoms such as headaches and stomach aches, difficulty sleeping, and bedwetting, as well as emotional effects such as depression, anxiety, insecurity, poor self-esteem, and even suicidal thoughts or behaviours.[24]

These harmful consequences do not only result from direct forms of bullying. Indirect bullying (e.g., relational, reputational, social, psychological) can also damage a person's sense of self, self-esteem, and social status, particularly for girls. Victims of indirect aggression might experience confusion at first, feeling unsure of what is happening to them. Other effects often follow, including psychological pain, distress, fear, and intimidation, problems with adjustment, and feelings of loneliness and isolation as well as depression in adulthood. Not infrequently, victims transfer to a new school to escape the bullying, or even contemplate suicide. Victimization sometimes worsens due to a cycle in which the emotional, physical, and social effects leave children more vulnerable to further bullying.[25]

Involvement in bullying is universally associated with negative school experiences. Victimized children describe themselves as unpopular, unhappy, powerless, afraid, and unsafe at school. They report avoiding school more often and may become less motivated. This can be accompanied by deteriorating grades. Strong connections and positive relationships among students and teachers may buffer the negative impact of bullying.[26]

We also need to be concerned about children who bully. They are more likely to be unhappy at school, have attention deficit disorder and depression, and to think about or attempt suicide. Youth who bully are more likely to use alcohol and drugs than their peers. Childhood aggression often continues into adolescence and may set the stage for delinquency, gang activity, criminal behaviour, and antisocial personality disorder. Even after controlling for other childhood risk factors, students involved in school bullying are significantly more likely to engage in criminal offending later in life. It is important to identify points at which early intervention can occur in order to change the life trajectories of aggressive children who perpetrate bullying and work toward preventing later violent and/or criminal behaviour.[27]

Bully-victims—those who are involved in situations as both a bully and a victim—appear to be particularly troubled. One population-based cohort study conducted in North Carolina examined adult psychiatric outcomes among four groups of individuals: those who had been bullied between ages 9 and 16, those who bullied others between those ages, those who were both bullies and victims at some point in that age range, and those never involved in bullying between those ages. Bullying was measured based on parent and child reports. Those individuals who were bully-victims in early adolescence had the highest levels of suicidality, depressive disorder, generalized anxiety disorder, and panic disorder in young adulthood. When controlling for childhood psychiatric issues and family hardships, bully-victims were still at significant risk for depressive disorders and for panic disorders, and male bully-victims were still at risk of suicidality. While we cannot conclude that involvement in bullying *causes* poor psychiatric outcomes in adulthood, these findings do highlight the significant issues that plague young people who both bully and are victimized. Individuals identified as victims and bully-victims in this study differed from those not involved in bullying in terms of their family background and their childhood psychological functioning. For these individuals, bullying occurred in the context of other risk factors, perhaps worsening an already deleterious situation. Early prevention and intervention efforts are key in addressing bullying as well as the spectrum of other issues with which such young people likely struggle (Copeland et al. 2013).

Concluding Comments

Bullying clearly affects children and adolescents around the world. There is consensus in the literature about certain issues, such as the need to employ a holistic and complex framework to understand and address bullying. Several issues continue to ignite controversy, including the definition of bullying and the degree of seriousness of various forms of bullying. Bullying threatens the rights of young people and can have serious long-term effects. We must remember that it can cause considerable and far-reaching damage for those who bully and are victimized. Adults have a responsibility to recognize all forms of bullying as serious and to listen to the perspectives of the young people involved in such incidents.

The presence and availability of positive and supportive adults can be very protective for young people in many respects, and can give children and youth the courage and coping skills to navigate complex bullying situations.

Chapter 2

Cyberbullying

Introduction

Over the past several decades, bullying has been recognized as a significant problem, attracting ever more research interest. Chapter 1 explored bullying as a form of aggression within a given relationship that may be direct or indirect, and may encompass a variety of behaviours. Cyberbullying,[1] however, is a more recent phenomenon; research is underway across the globe—in Australia, Belgium, Canada, Czech Republic, England, Israel, Italy, Singapore, the United States, as well as other countries.[2]

This chapter provides an overview of cyberbullying, with particular focus on Canadian research and policy. Cyberbullying can only be understood in the context in which it occurs: the cyber world. For this reason, we will discuss the nature of the cyber world and its significant meaning for young people. We will then provide an overview of what we currently know about cyberbullying. Throughout, we discuss how it is both similar to and different from traditional, face-to-face bullying forms. We conclude with a discussion focused on responding to cyberbullying.

Definition of Cyberbullying

There is little consensus on what constitutes cyberbullying. This is likely a reflection of its complexity and the fact that it is a relatively new phenomenon. It may be similar in some respects to traditional bullying, with comparable negative emotional, social, and psychological effects. But questions arise. Should we label it cyberbullying if it does not have some of the elements of traditional bullying, such as power imbalance, intentionality, and repetition? It remains unclear whether to categorize it as an electronic form of bullying or as a distinct phenomenon. It is also unclear whether children, youth, parents, teachers, clinicians, and researchers refer to similar definitions of cyberbullying. In any case, definitional clarity is a necessary first step.

Broadly speaking, cyberbullying may be defined as the use of technology to *bully* another person, which results in harm or negative consequences for the victim. Recall our discussion in Chapter 1 about how to define bullying. Bullying typically involves one or more persons intentionally using aggression toward another person(s) with less power, and this aggression is often repeated over time. When this kind of aggressive behaviour is displayed in the cyber world, we consider it cyberbullying. Sameer Hinduja and Justin Patchin have offered a similar definition of cyberbullying. They define it as "willful and repeated harm inflicted through the use of computers, cell phones, and other electronic devices" (Hinduja & Patchin 2009, 5). This definition highlights bullying behaviour as not only deliberate, but also as taking place over time and reflecting a pattern. Another key aspect of this definition is that the victim is hurt or harmed in some way by the behaviour.

The definition offered by Hinduja and Patchin is a useful starting point for our discussion. Importantly, however, we must point out that there is great debate in the literature regarding definitions. To illuminate the complexity of defining cyberbullying, let's return to the example provided in Chapter 1. Here, a girl discreetly photographs an overweight classmate in the locker room and emails it to her best friend, who then distributes the photo to a much larger audience. In this example, the girl deliberately took the photo and deliberately sent it to her best friend. She did not intend for the photo to be widely distributed, however. Further, this may be the first time the girl has done something like this. Neither of these factors excuses her behaviour, nor do they necessarily change how we might interpret this action; it may well still be an incident of cyberbullying. Even if this were atypical behaviour for the girl, and even if the incident does not constitute an identifiable pattern of behaviour, the harm to her classmate was indeed repeated. Her best friend repeated the aggressive behaviour by circulating the photo, and the victim suffered harm each and every time another person accessed it. Furthermore, the victim had no way of ensuring that the photo could ever be permanently deleted from the cyber world. Since it is a digital image, it can be reproduced and distributed with ease to an unlimited number of viewers. Who are the perpetrators in this situation? The original photographer? Her best friend? Peers who participated in ridiculing the victim by accessing the photo? Strangers who later accessed the image after it was more widely distributed in cyberspace? The complexity of these questions contributes to definitional confusion.

Another difficulty in arriving at a clear definition of cyberbullying results from the wide array of aggressive behaviours that can take place within the cyber world, not to mention how rapidly this world continues to evolve. Given these many complexities, cyberbullying cannot be defined by any single identifiable behaviour on any single technological device. Like traditional bullying, it can encompass a variety of behaviours, such as rumour spreading, direct insults or threats, or manipulating friendships. It can also involve inviting others to physically harm an individual in the offline world, or distributing images or videos of someone being beat up at school. Also like traditional bullying, determining whether a particular incident constitutes cyberbullying can be problematic. For instance, logging into a friend's Facebook account and posting embarrassing content may be cyberbullying in some contexts, but it could be interpreted as a joke among friends in others. To assess whether the situation described above constitutes cyberbullying, we should primarily focus on the victim's interpretation of the event, while also considering the other elements of traditional face-to-face forms of bullying, such as the intent to cause harm and power imbalance.[3]

Assessing the intent to cause harm in situations of cyberbullying is not always easy. In the above example, for instance, did the girl who took the photo of her overweight classmate intend to bring harm to that classmate? While we can be fairly sure that her best friend intended to hurt her peer, the photographer's intentions are unclear. She clearly wanted to mock her peer, even though she "only" meant to share this with her best friend. Consider an offline example in which a young person draws a cartoonish doodle of an overweight classmate, with her weight greatly exaggerated, her name written on the cartoon, and the caption, "Ew!" The teen might only share it with her best friend and no one else ever finds out about it. How should adults respond in the online and offline versions of this scenario? Both on- and offline, while the creator of the images may not have intended to directly hurt her peer, she clearly did intend to mock her. In both scenarios, this girl's behaviour needs to be addressed. In the cyber example, a stronger response would likely be necessary to ensure that the photographer understands the potentially broad impact of her actions, and the hurt it has caused her peer, in order to prevent her from doing something like this again. This does not necessarily imply that a more punitive response is required; rather, the situation calls for all parties to be cognizant of the fact that the cyber scenario resulted in significantly more harm to a young person, which must be taken into account.

The power imbalance typically present in traditional bullying may appear in cases of cyberbullying and may be based on similar factors. Although it is commonly believed that cyberbullying occurs largely anonymously, most incidents occur in the context of a relationship, just like traditional forms. The factors that determine who holds more power in the face-to-face world may therefore translate to the cyber world. The most popular girl in the classroom might hold power over her less popular peers both at school and online. Likewise, the teenage boy who identifies as gay might hold less power than his heterosexual peers in both the face-to-face and cyber worlds. Other factors that may determine power include race, gender, socio-economic status, religion, ability, physical size, and social skills.

Unique to incidents of cyberbullying, technological access and skill might determine who holds the most power in any given situation online. Further, the nature of the cyber world may encourage young people to be bolder and less prudent, which might in turn lessen any power imbalance that exists in the offline world. That is, the perception of anonymity provided by the online world, coupled with the reduced inhibitions it can promote, might actually embolden children and youth who hold less power in the offline world to engage in cyberbullying, or empower victims to "fight back." To be clear, we do not see this empowerment as a benefit of the cyber world. Rather, while the nature of the cyber world can equalize power relations, it can also encourage retaliation and escalating aggression among peers.[4]

It is clear that there are similarities between traditional bullying and cyberbullying. Cyber forms, however, can be distinguished from traditional forms in numerous ways. Cyberbullying can occur day and night, across geographical and even national boundaries; in other words, victimization can take place beyond traditional borders. Moreover, it is no longer confined to the school day. Another key distinction is the actual or perceived anonymity that comes with the cyber world. Although most often the perpetrator and victim are known to one another and have some existing relationship, it is possible for perpetrators to remain relatively anonymous, at least for a period of time. Further, with traditional bullying, witnesses are limited in number. Cyberbullying incidents, by contrast, may involve an unlimited number of possible witnesses. And as we noted above, the content is far more reproducible; text or images can be distributed very quickly to a wide audience.[5]

Consider the "Star Wars Kid" incident. Ghyslain Raza was a high school student from Quebec who filmed himself swinging a piece of sports equipment around like a lightsaber (hence, the name that he has been given). In 2003, classmates found the tape and made fun of the boy, originally distributing it among a few friends but later uploading it to the Internet, all without Raza's knowledge or consent. What followed was devastating for Raza. *Maclean's* magazine has called him "one of the earliest and highest-profile victims of a massive cyber bullying attack, one that played out among classmates and strangers online" ("10 Years

Later" 2013). Given that the cyber world was not yet as advanced, it is unlikely that the students who originally uploaded the video intended for it to go "viral." But it appears the original intention was to mock Raza, clearly in line with what we think of as bullying. Once the online world became involved, the perpetrators grew in numbers and ferociousness. Raza recalls becoming the target of both spite and violence. He was even told to commit suicide. He also became a victim of traditional, face-to-face bullying as a result of the video. He had to change schools, he lost his friends, and he describes feeling worthless. To date, the first copy of the video posted on YouTube has over 28 million views. It remains accessible on the Internet in many formats.

The "Star Wars Kid" incident sheds light on some important differences between traditional and cyberbullying. Before the development of the cyber world, the original perpetrators might have watched the video of Raza, perhaps showed it to a few friends. The perpetrators might have tormented Raza at school, using both direct and indirect aggression. In a fairly severe scenario, Raza might have changed schools to get a fresh start in a place where no one knew about the video. In all likelihood, he would have received the fresh start he desired. In actuality, this was not possible for Raza. Since this incident occurred in the digital age, there is everlasting documentation of his humiliation. Ten years later, he can still search "Star Wars Kid" and find millions of hits that focus on an incident that he experienced as incredibly hurtful and humiliating. At the time of writing, the search term "Star Wars Kid" returned over 32 million results on Google.

The original perpetrators also faced serious consequences as a result of this incident. The Raza family sought $351,000 in damages from the parents of the three students who allegedly posted the video online and labelled the teen the "Star Wars Kid" ("Star Wars Kid" 2006). The case was eventually settled out of court. It is unlikely this lawsuit would have been pursued if this incident had occurred prior to the digital age, as the harm inflicted on Raza would have been much less severe. As one can imagine, it was nearly impossible to hold all of Raza's tormenters accountable. They existed both in his school and around the world. The three students named as the original perpetrators were held accountable, although it could be argued that they unfairly bore the brunt of a situation that went far beyond them. The "Star Wars Kid" incident truly exemplifies how challenging it can be to identify and respond fairly to cyberbullying situations, all the while considering the feelings of the victim, the intentions of the perpetrators, and the spiralling or magnifying effect that can occur in the cyber world.

The Cyber World

The dramatic technological advances that have occurred in recent history have forever changed the ways that we communicate and interact. Canadians have unreservedly embraced the always-advancing cyber world, which includes social networking sites (e.g., Facebook, Twitter, Tumblr, Pinterest), YouTube, email, and webcams, all of which can be accessed through a personal computer or smart phone. Computers, smart phones, and other electronic devices have been called the tools of the cyberbully. The accessibility of these tools makes it much easier to act aggressively toward others (Hinduja & Patchin 2009). These tools are ingrained in the daily lives of Canadians. We cannot ignore or underestimate their importance (and that of the cyber world to which they give us access) to children, youth, and adults alike. The cyber world inevitably interacts with and mutually influences other important social environments like the home, the school, and the community (Johnson & Puplampu 2008; Martin & Stuart 2011). We now develop and maintain relationships in the cyber world with peers, friends, neighbours, co-workers, and others. Knowing that bullying occurs in the context of relationships, it is not surprising that cyber forms of bullying have developed.

The current generation of children and youth has never experienced a world without technology. Less than 10 years ago, social networking and video sites were not widely known or available. Today, they are ubiquitous. In Canada, 98 percent of youth access the Internet and use information and communication technologies on a daily basis, and the age at which children engage in the cyber world keeps getting younger. An example is the YouTube video "A magazine is an iPad that does not work," in which an infant uses an iPad with ease. The child is then given a magazine and attempts to make the pages "work," using hand motions that would typically be used to operate the iPad. As the YouTube subscriber who posted the video writes, "technology codes our minds, changes our OS."[6]

As any adult having grown up prior to the digital age knows, children and youth are sophisticated users of technology and acquire technological competence at a much faster rate than their parents. Youth are able to keep up with constant and rapid technological advances, contributing to a clear and unmistakable generational divide. It can sometimes appear to young people that adults are oblivious to their conduct online, including cyberbullying behaviours. Many youth in fact engage with the online world without adult supervision and often without their parents' knowledge. The generational divide, as well as the perception that parents and teachers are not monitoring conduct, can set the stage for young people to engage in behaviours they might otherwise refrain from in the presence of adults. It is in this context that cyberbullying occurs. We must remember that children and youth may not be able to use technology in appropriate ways, even though they can certainly utilize it with technical sophistication. As with any other developmental task, young people require adult guidance and support in order to learn how to use technology in a responsible manner.[7]

While we must recognize the new social issues that have emerged for children and youth as a result of the cyber world, we must also remember that recent technological advances have provided us with immense benefits. Today, information and communication technologies are accessed by Canadians for a variety of purposes, including education, information, social connection, entertainment, and personal assistance and growth. This technology is rapidly advancing each and every day, and for this reason it has outpaced legislators, politicians, and parents across the country—and around the world—who are trying to figure out how to take the best from this new technology while minimizing its risks.

The cyber world provides young people with unprecedented opportunities to communicate with others both in and out of their existing face-to-face social networks. Youth can interact with people from around the world, creating opportunities for cross-cultural exchanges, education, and identity development. This engagement is constant, transcending the boundaries of time and space. In the cyber world, youth have access to social supports, both informally through relationships with friends, and formally through counselling and online therapeutic resources.

The risks associated with the cyber world go beyond cyberbullying. Other issues of concern for parents, educators, and policy makers include sexual solicitation or victimization, and exposure to harmful material such as pornography, violent images, or hate messages. Although this chapter focuses exclusively on cyberbullying among peers, it is worth noting that there will be overlap among the different forms of cyber risk.[8] With these risks in mind, parents often try to regulate their children's technology use. This can be a daunting task, particularly with the increase in mobile media use in recent years. It seems clear that monitoring alone cannot protect our children and youth from the risks of the cyber world. We must accept that young people will exercise autonomy and agency in the cyber world. We must prepare them to behave responsibly and appropriately, while also attempting to monitor their activities. Most importantly, we must work to establish and maintain open lines of communication with young people about both the positive and negative interactions they have in the cyber world. With open communication in place, young people will be more willing to come to an adult for help if they experience or witness concerning situations online such as cyberbullying (Bumpus & Werner 2009).

The Complexity of the Online Experience

Navigating social relationships in the cyber world is not always easy, a fact that is true for youth and adults alike. Several inherent features of the cyber world affect us in certain ways and influence the way we interact with others. These effects can increase the likelihood that cyberbullying will occur and can also intensify the harmful impact of this bullying.

- Communicating in the cyber world can lower inhibitions and increase spontaneity
- The cyber world affords individuals the *perception* of anonymity
- There are fewer social cues in the cyber world
- Individuals often lack understanding of consequences for their cyber actions
- There is a permanent record of events in the cyber world
- The cyber world is available to us anytime and anywhere

The cyber world allows for spontaneous, frequent, and instant communication with others. As we saw above, it also tends to have a disinhibiting effect on people. This can be a dangerous combination that leads children and youth to engage in impulsive behaviours in which they otherwise would not participate. This disinhibition effect could derive from the perception of anonymity that the cyber world affords, or from the lack of apparent and immediate consequences of certain negative behaviours online. For instance, it is relatively simple to create a new email or social media account in order to bully a peer with apparent anonymity. Let's consider a 17-year-old girl who has just had a falling out with her best friend. Feeling hurt and angry, she gets home from school and in a rage decides to create a fake Facebook account to send angry messages to her former best friend, such as, "I am going to tell everyone at school that you are a slut and that you slept with that 25-year-old last summer!" She might think there is no way she could get "in trouble" for this behaviour because she will never be identified as the sender. Ironically, nothing is truly anonymous in the cyber world, and the presence of a record of bullying incidents actually makes this behaviour much more incriminating than traditional forms. Furthermore, the target will likely be able to identify the "anonymous" perpetrator based on shared knowledge.

There are fewer social cues and norms in the cyber world when compared to the offline world. Take a moment to consider the significant influence of social cues and norms in daily life. We constantly "read" the body language, vocal inflections, and facial expressions of others around us. We can easily tell when someone "clams up" and doesn't want to talk about a topic, or when another is overjoyed about some good news. We also have grown up in a context where there are countless social norms that guide our behaviour. For instance, when a colleague asks, "How are you?" the appropriate answer is most often "Good" or "Fine." In the cyber world, many of the cues and norms to which we usually have access are absent. This can create a situation in which we become less sensitive and empathetic to the feelings of others, because we do not have our usual cues to spark these feelings. We are also more likely to misinterpret or misunderstand the feelings and intentions of others in this context. A teen might misinterpret a joke sent by a friend through text message, thinking her friend is being rude and disrespectful. A child may make fun of another constantly over Facebook without realizing the impact of this behaviour. In a face-to-face context, the expression of hurt on the victim's face may have been enough for the child to stop making fun.[9]

Despite proficiency with technology, youth rarely have a realistic understanding of the consequences of their online actions. For instance, our research found that only a small minority of youth knew that after posting content online, it could not be completely removed. Children and youth must be made aware of this key fact, which may encourage them to think twice before posting material. For instance, consider a 12-year-old who alters a photograph of an unpopular classmate so that there are insults written all around the person, like, "You are so stupid and fat!" and then posts this on Instagram. This photograph can never be completely removed, and it can be distributed widely and easily, far beyond the perpetrator's Instagram feed. The victim in this scenario will be faced with this image for a long time after it is posted, the harm associated with the bullying potentially reverberating and staying with the victim. As we saw above with Ghyslain Raza, online bullying can so easily cross the boundaries of time and space that escaping it may feel impossible. The perpetrator will likely also face long-term consequences, perhaps in the coming years as he matures and it becomes less socially acceptable to ridicule others.[10]

What We Know about Cyberbullying

Prevalence rates of cyberbullying typically range from about 10 percent to 40 percent of children and youth,[11] while other research reports higher rates.[12] There is significant variability in prevalence estimates, due in part to inconsistent definitions and methodological approaches used across studies. Recently, several researchers attempted to account for these differences and inconsistencies by conducting a meta-analytic review of 131 cross-sectional cyberbullying studies (Kowalski et al. 2014). While the cross-sectional nature of the 131 studies eliminates any possibility of determining cause-effect relationships, this meta-analysis does identify several risk and protective factors for both cyber victimization and cyberbullying. The findings reveal a strong relationship between experiencing cyber victimization and perpetrating cyberbullying, suggesting that young people may often be involved as both a bully and victim in the cyber context. There also appears to be a connection between involvement in traditional bullying, as both a bully and victim, and an increased risk of involvement in cyberbullying. Factors that may offer protection from becoming involved in cyberbullying as a perpetrator and/or victim include school safety, positive school climate, and parental monitoring.

Based on this meta-analysis as well as other research, there appears to be considerable overlap between traditional and cyberbullying. The young people who are at greatest risk of victimization in the cyber world appear to be those who are also at greatest risk in the offline world, and vice versa. Children and youth who are involved in bullying at school are likely to retain their roles as bully or victim in the context of the cyber world, but may also shift roles (from victim in the offline context to perpetrator in the online context, or vice versa). Perhaps the involvement begins in the cyber world and continues at school, or perhaps bullying begins at school and continues online. In either case, there are important implications of this overlap. With bullying no longer confined to the school day, involvement has intensified for both bullies and victims.

Youth may be involved in both traditional and cyberbullying as perpetrators, victims, or bully-victims (i.e., both a victim and a perpetrator of bullying). Research on traditional bullying typically reports that compared to those who are perpetrators and are victimized, there are relatively fewer young people who fit in the category of bully-victim. Research has also found that those who do fit in this category are particularly troubled. Our research alongside other Canadian studies suggests that in the cyber world, more young people are bully-victims than in traditional bullying, and that it is generally more difficult to distinguish bullies from victims and witnesses in cyber interactions. It may be easier to engage in reciprocal bullying in the cyber world, where victims can quickly retaliate and bystanders can be drawn into aggressive interactions. This blurs the role distinctions among perpetrators, victims, and bystanders.[13]

Relationship Context and Importance of Bystanders

Cyberbullying typically occurs in the context of relationships. The fact that it is not solely characterized by anonymity suggests that it may be understood as a relationship issue. It is also consistent with the fact that most youth use technology to communicate with others they already know.

According to our research, one-quarter of cyberbullying occurs in the presence of witnesses. As in traditional bullying, witnesses to these incidents are largely peers of those involved, and these peers play key roles. Other research has found that between one-half and two-thirds of youth respondents have witnessed cyberbullying incidents. The matter of witnesses merits special attention. The boundary between witness and participant is easily blurred in the cyber world. Even though a given teen may not have created aggressive and hurtful text or images, if he or she views or spreads that content, it constitutes participation. Indeed, research suggests that negative bystander behaviour (i.e., participating in an incident of bullying by acting aggressively toward the target) is more likely to occur in the cyber context compared to the face-to-face world.

It is imperative that education and interventions focus on promoting positive bystander behaviour, to encourage young people to identify the characteristics of problematic situations and stand up for peers when they witness such situations. For instance, educators could focus on teaching children and youth why it is hurtful to create and post an image of an unpopular classmate with accompanying insults, why it is wrong to reproduce and further distribute this image, and why this image should be reported as inappropriate.

It is also important to teach children and youth about the lack of privacy in the cyber world. A young person may believe that privately sharing an insult-laced photograph with only one friend involves limited harm. Clearly, this belief may not match the outcome. It is important to teach children and youth that aside from the behaviour being problematic in and of itself, there are no guarantees that it will remain private in the cyber world. It is easy to talk about the importance of this type of education, but effective implementation that can change the behaviour of children and youth is another matter. The entire group context and online milieu must change in order to truly facilitate positive bystander behaviour among individual children and adolescents. Otherwise, this behaviour can feel—or, in fact, it may well actually be—too risky.

Empathy is an important concept that can help us promote positive cyber bystander behaviour. In one study, researchers showed a two-minute video about cyberbullying to a group of adolescents, in which the victim's feelings and the effects on her behaviour were clearly depicted. Then, researchers assessed bystander behaviour by asking participants to choose a response after receiving a message from a peer that mocked another classmate. For the cyber scenario, participants could choose to forward the message to a peer or add it to a public online forum, or alternatively they could choose to delete it. In the traditional, face-to-face scenario, participants could choose to pass the message to another student or put it up in the school hallway, or alternatively to throw it away. Interestingly, watching the video led to a change in the emotional state of those who viewed it, suggesting that the viewers felt empathy for the victim. Further, those teenagers who watched the video, compared to those who did not, were significantly less likely to engage in negative bystander behaviour. This negative behaviour was also less likely when young people were encouraged to identify with the situation depicted in the video and to focus on the aspects that reflected the victim's emotions and behaviours. These findings have important practical implications. By working to increase empathy for victims of cyberbullying, we can potentially discourage children and youth from acting as negative bystanders in cyberbullying situations.[14]

Gender

It is unclear whether gender affects the involvement of young people in cyberbullying, and in which contexts it might do so.[15] We found several differences in the cyberbullying involvement of boys and girls in our research. While boys and girls were equally likely to report when they had cyberbullied others, the type of cyberbullying experienced and perpetrated varied by gender. Our findings highlighted that gender differences in cyberbullying correspond with well-documented differences in traditional bullying, with boys more involved in direct forms and girls more involved in indirect forms. For instance, girls were more likely than boys to have had rumours spread about them online. On the other hand, boys in grades 10 and 11 were more likely to have been threatened online compared to girls of the same age. When girls experienced direct victimization, it tended to be of a sexual nature. For example, girls in grades 10 and 11 were more likely than boys to be sent unwelcome sexual pictures or texts, to be asked to do something sexual online (e.g., asked to send a sexual photo of themselves), and to have had their private photos distributed online without their consent. The perpetrators in these incidents were typically boys. Other studies, including our focus groups, confirm the sexual harassment and sexualized bullying faced by girls in the cyber setting.[16]

Impact of Cyberbullying

Cyberbullying can be distressing for young people, and it is of growing concern for parents, educators, and society. Students who are cyberbullied report feeling sad, anxious, afraid, and unable to concentrate on school, and they may experience social difficulties and eating disorders. Victimized youth are more likely to skip school, be given detentions or suspensions, or take a weapon to school. In addition, these young people may use substances, engage in unsafe sexual practices, and display violent or suicidal behaviour. Perpetrators are less likely to show empathy and may struggle with low self-esteem, depression, and problem behaviours such as substance use and delinquency.

Involvement in cyberbullying as a perpetrator or as a victim affects the well-being of youth, and in some situations it may impact young people above and beyond the effects of traditional bullying. A study of youth in grades 8 through 10 in British Columbia found that involvement as a perpetrator or victim was a predictor of depressive symptoms and suicidal ideation, over and above the effect of traditional bullying involvement.

Cyberbullying may be more frightening than traditional bullying, particularly because it is hard to escape from it. Most individuals remain socially connected online; the primary escape route would be to sever this connection. This is rarely a viable option. While parents can limit access to the cyber world and monitor activities, it is unrealistic to think that children and youth can simply press the "off" button to avoid cyberbullying. As we have already discussed, the cyber world has enormous benefits and is truly a lifeline to social relationships for all Canadians, particularly youth.[17]

As with traditional bullying, young people tend to avoid disclosing experiences of cyberbullying. Indeed, disclosing cyberbullying to an adult is the least common coping strategy identified by youth. According to our survey findings, more than half of the participants who reported being cyberbullied said that they did nothing in response, and few participants chose to tell a parent or teacher. Young people may fear that disclosure will result in loss of access to their computers, smart phones, and other digital devices. In our focus groups, participants were adamant that despite their parents' good intentions, losing digital access felt like punishment. It is a reasonable assumption, however, that not disclosing incidents of cyberbullying delays receiving help. For this reason, it is essential that teachers and other school personnel, along with parents, understand how to promote disclosure and respond appropriately upon learning of cyberbullying involvement.[18]

Responding to Cyberbullying

As a nation, we must respond to cyberbullying to ensure that the rights of children and youth are promoted and protected. We all share responsibility for preventing and intervening in cases of cyberbullying, and we cannot expect any individual parent, youth, researcher, teacher, or policy maker to address this issue in its entirety. Strategies for responding to cyberbullying must involve the coordinated efforts of individuals, schools, and communities, as well as representatives from all levels of government. There is no single solution to cyberbullying, and therefore multiple tools and resources need to be utilized in order to increase the effectiveness of prevention and intervention efforts.

A basic first step involves understanding the perspectives of youth and the importance of the online world in their social lives. It is essential that adults take a non-judgmental stance toward young people who engage with the cyber world, and that they maintain open lines of communication. Adults must be viewed as safe havens for youth so that if young people experience troubling situations online, they feel comfortable discussing these experiences with trusted adults in their lives, with little fear of judgment or loss of privileges. Researchers, educators, parents, and policy makers must fully understand the new language of the cyber world in order to narrow the generational gap. Another important initial step is recognizing that technology is not to blame for cyberbullying. Rather, bullying is embedded in relational issues and, for the contemporary generation, relationships evolve within the cyber world.

There are many excellent Canadian resources for young people, parents, and educators on responding to cyberbullying. The WITS program (Walk away, Ignore, Talk it out, and Seek help; www.witsprogram.ca) website contains several useful resources, such as guidelines to help parents become involved in their children's cyber lives. Suggestions include learning everything about children's online behaviour and discussing the importance of treating others with kindness and respect in the cyber world. The WITS website also contains links to a wealth of resources, such as www. commonsensemedia.org, a website that contains free downloads for apps related to cyberbullying prevention and intervention, among other useful things.

Another excellent Canadian resource, Media Smarts (www.mediasmarts.ca), is a centre for digital and media literacy, containing general information to help boost literacy as well as information on specific issues and phenomena including cyberbullying. This website offers up-to-date links to research and policy documents, as well as exceptional resources for educators, including full lesson plans, workshops, and tutorials. The website also offers detailed information on the current efforts of each province and territory to provide media education.

As introduced in Chapter 1, the PREVNet website (www.prevnet.ca) is an extremely valuable resource for information on all forms of bullying, including cyberbullying. A definition of cyberbullying is offered and its harmful consequences are discussed. Lesson plans and tip sheets are available to help educators and parents address and confront cyberbullying. Practical strategies are offered, encouraging parents to listen to their children, report incidents of cyberbullying to the school, and document any problematic activity to show Internet service providers and police if necessary. Also included are helpful strategies for parents of children who cyberbully others. Parents of such youth are encouraged to keep computers in a common area, to charge children's cellphones in the parents' room overnight, and to set up social media and other accounts together with children in order to continuously monitor their contacts.

Justin Patchin and Sameer Hinduja are co-directors of the US-based *Cyberbullying Research Center* (www.cyberbullying.us), another helpful resource, which serves as a clearinghouse of information on the ways young people use and misuse technology. Handouts for teens include "A Student's Guide to Personal Publishing," a critical document for young people that outlines issues to consider before publishing content online. In a teen-friendly manner, Patchin and Hinduja point out that anything published online can eventually be read and seen by anyone, and that it is permanently recorded in the cyber world, which can have repercussions if anything inappropriate, embarrassing, or hurtful to others is posted. They also highlight that although it appears possible to publish content anonymously online using pseudonyms and aliases, just about everything published can be traced back to a specific person's digital footprint. Patchin and Hinduja also provide "top ten tips" for parents and educators for preventing and responding to cyberbullying. They encourage parents to first and foremost make sure children feel safe, secure, and unconditionally supported. Parents are also encouraged to thoroughly investigate situations in order to understand all of the complexities of cyberbullying incidents. The website includes a number of other helpful suggestions for parents and educators.

A unique and particularly helpful component of the *Cyberbullying Research Center* is a space for young people, parents, and educators to share their stories about cyberbullying. These stories are then used to educate others about cyberbullying, with the ultimate goal of preventing it from occurring in the future. Recall the research findings on empathy and cyberbullying: narratives that depict the impact of victimization can actually prevent children and youth from engaging in negative bystander behaviour (e.g., forwarding a private picture that was distributed without the consent of the person depicted). Allowing victims to share their stories may also be experienced as empowering, and may help reduce feelings of isolation and stigmatization.

One story submitted by a 13-year-old girl from the United States reads, "There's a game called habbo.com. Now there's a certain room in there called chromide club where the kids go to make fun of people. It's bad because they get your Facebook and make fun of the way u look. They spam your Facebook throughout the game and it hurts people's feelings."

A 15-year-old boy from the United States wrote, "I was on Facebook when a friend of mine wrote on my wall that whenever I was in someone's life their life started to get fucked up. That hurt a lot because I trusted this person. He verbally bullies me whenever he gets the chance. I don't want to tell my mom because she'll make a big deal about it. I'm really getting hurt from this. Why does he have to be a wimp and say it online and not to my face? He'd be a man if he did."

The mother of a 14-year-old girl wrote, "Some girl in my daughter's grade started a rumor that my daughter is a lesbian, this got all over school, not happy with that she starting texting her with all this comments. I spoke to her mom and ask her to please make her stop. Well big mistake … she post comments on Facebook, mocking her. We will start counseling very soon, I'm afraid for my daughter's safety, not sure how bad this is affecting her, and she tells me that she's trying to avoid them in school. This is a terrible experience that no child should have to go thru."

There are thousands more. These represent the words and feelings of people who have been affected by cyberbullying. The posts shed light on what is happening right now, "on the ground," and how we can go about preventing and responding to situations of cyberbullying.[19]

Public Policy and Legal Responses to Cyberbullying

There is a range of tensions in public policy responses to cyberbullying, including freedom of speech, privacy, best interests of the child, and parental and school protective responsibilities. The legal ramifications of cyberbullying are often unclear, given that there is rarely an obvious distinction between behaviours that are right and wrong. For instance, there have been a number of recent cases in the media in which traditional or cyberbullying has been cited as a cause of youth suicide. Suicide is complex, however, and treating bullying of either kind as the sole cause is an oversimplification. More likely there will have been a combination of factors, such as mental health issues, family difficulties, substance use, marginalization, and bullying. While experiences of cyberbullying may be one contributor to suicide, it is hard to disentangle its role when combined with additional vulnerabilities.[20]

Advances in technology have far outpaced policy and legal guidelines regarding cyber behaviour. Further research is needed on a range of questions: How law attaches or should attach liability to the emotional harm caused by words or images in cyber space; how law attaches or should attach liability for participating in various capacities in bullying online, or in offline incidents with online elements (e.g., participating as an instigator or bystander, participating by posting or distributing an image or video of an offline incident); and how law attaches or should attach liability for offline incidents instigated by online activities (e.g., suicide following cyberbullying involvement). A fact worth remembering is that technology is constantly advancing, and so cyberbullying may be expressed quite differently in the coming years, months, and even weeks. Its definition in law and policy must therefore be precise, but not restricted to a named set of behaviours that are expressed on a named set of technological devices.[21]

At this time, there are several potential legal remedies for cyberbullying in Canada, including school sanctions, criminal and tort liability, and human rights legislation. Similar remedies can be applied in the United States, with similar issues and complexities associated with their application.

School sanctions

The school context is key in understanding and addressing cyberbullying, because even though it often takes place outside of school it frequently occurs within the context of school-based relationships, and it may begin at school and continue online, or vice versa.[22] Canadian school boards are responsible for providing safe learning environments for the children in their care and have tools such as suspension and expulsion to address code of conduct violations.[23] Importantly, many provincial education acts were written before the cyber world existed, and thus do not necessarily apply to situations of cyberbullying. Unlike traditional bullying, the consequences of cyberbullying usually involve psychological rather than physical harm, and the actual incidents often take place outside of school. These distinctions create complications when school officials attempt to use provincial education acts to impose discipline in relation to cyberbullying. To address this issue, several provinces have enacted or are currently preparing legislation that obliges school boards to confront bullying and cyberbullying, even when it occurs off school grounds, in cases when it contributes to a negative environment at school.

In Ontario, the Education Act was updated in 2012 with Bill 13, the "Accepting Schools Act," which defines cyberbullying and requires school boards to promote prevention as well as establish discipline guidelines for perpetrators.[24] The Quebec Education Act was amended in June 2012, such that the definition of bullying now includes activities conducted in cyberspace, and the governing boards of schools are required to create anti-bullying plans that address cyber incidents. Alberta passed amendments to its Education Act in 2012 in order to include psychological harm and harm to a person's reputation in the definition of bullying.[25] Students in Alberta are required to refrain from bullying and report instances of it, regardless of whether it occurs on school grounds, during school hours, or through electronic means.[26] In Saskatchewan, although specific legislation does not yet exist, a province-wide Anti-Bullying Strategy has been announced. In 2013, Manitoba amended its Public Schools Act to explicitly include cyber-bullying as unacceptable conduct in its schools,[27] and the Northwest Territories enacted anti-cyberbullying legislation modelled on the Ontario acts.[28] New Brunswick's Education Act was also amended in 2012 to include cyberbullying in the definition of serious misconduct.[29]

In Nova Scotia, the Promotion of Respectful and Responsible Relationships Act was enacted in late 2012, modifying the Education Act to include cyberbullying as an example of disruptive behaviour. This occurred in response to several high-profile suicides in which cyberbullying was believed to be a contributing factor. In early 2013, the Cyber-Safety Act was also introduced in Nova Scotia, which strengthened the Education Act to allow school officials to discipline off-campus behaviour that disrupts the learning climate of the school.[30]

In summary, legislative changes have recently been enacted in the provinces of Ontario, Quebec, Alberta, Nova Scotia, Manitoba, New Brunswick, and the Northwest Territories to address cyberbullying through the school. At the time of writing, other provinces and territories in Canada have not yet enacted this type of legislation, although most Education Acts now address bullying and cyberbullying at some level in statutes, regulations, and/or policies.

Criminal liability

In Canada, criminal law is a federal power administered by the provinces. The federal Criminal Code contains a number of provisions that may be applicable in cases of bullying or cyberbullying, such as harassment and assault, although many cyberbullying behaviours are not captured in the legal definitions of these crimes.[31] As a result, the Justice Minister introduced the Protecting Canadians from Online Crime Act (Bill C-13) in November

2013. Among other items, this bill will make it a crime to transmit intimate images of a person without their knowledge or consent.[32]

Several prominent cases have involved the distribution of intimate photographs, and when the photographs involve a minor, child pornography laws may be applied. Crown prosecutors have been reluctant to apply child pornography charges in cases of cyberbullying, however, as these situations are often very different from what we might think of as the typical child pornography case. For instance, "sexting" or other forms of image distribution may occur among age-mate peers. In some cases, it may be consensual and remain private, only shared with and viewed by the intended audience. While this may not reflect the best judgment on the part of those involved, it is distinct from the situations in which peers distribute private images, without consent, to unintended audiences. Further, both of these scenarios are distinct from what we might call a typical child pornography case, in which an adult creates or distributes exploitative sexual images of children and adolescents, actions that are clearly pathological and inherently harmful to young people.

Cyberbullying behaviours are sometimes consistent with "defamatory libel"[33]—the crime of publishing false statements, without lawful justification or excuse, that are likely to injure the reputation of another person. Criminal prosecution of defamation, however, is rare.

Tort liability

A "tort" is a breach of a legal duty to another person, which is addressed by civil lawsuits between plaintiffs and defendants. As part of the Cyber-Safety Act in Nova Scotia, a new tort was created for cyberbullying, giving the courts in this province the power to award damages and to deliver a court order to refrain from engaging in the behaviour in the future.[34] Under this act, parents of cyberbullies who fail to take steps to prevent their children's behaviour from continuing can be held liable.[35] This represents the first law in Canada that makes cyberbullying a tort. In other provinces, the tort of defamation can be applied in some cases of cyberbullying, but many cases would fall outside the legal definition.

Human rights legislation

Canada's Human Rights Act and parallel provincial acts ensure that students are not discriminated against in their educational experience on the basis of race, national or ethnic origin, colour, religion, age, sex, sexual orientation, or disability.[36] This act also prohibits hate speech, or, in other words, public communications that expose a person to discriminatory hatred.[37] To date, there have been no Canada Human Rights Tribunals involving school-based bullying or cyberbullying, although in one case a young person successfully sued the school board under British Columbia's Human Rights Act after suffering years of homophobic bullying that negatively affected his educational experience.[38] Further discussion of human rights and bias-based bullying in the Canadian context will be presented in Chapter 3, in addition to comparisons with the United States.

Concluding Comments

Adults in Canada have a responsibility to protect children from all forms of physical and mental violence, injury, or abuse. The cyber world has many benefits for children and youth but it also presents risks. These risks signal an urgent call to action for adults to intervene in order to protect young people. Adults must recognize that the cyber world is equivalent to the social world for the current generation of children and youth, and that cyberbullying occurs within this context. When viewed as safe havens, adults can provide crucial support for young people in need. In the absence of a simple solution for cyberbullying and other forms of cyber risk, we need to evolve a multi-faceted approach.

Chapter 3

Bias-Based Bullying

Introduction

In Chapter 1, we introduced bias-based bullying as a pattern of behaviour motivated by intolerance toward others due to real or perceived aspects of their identity. This type of bullying may appear in any form and may stem from bias against another person based on gender, race, religion, sexual orientation, ability, and/or socio-economic status. It results from and reinforces discrimination toward minorities and other groups living in marginalized situations based on certain characteristics. In a country like Canada, it is particularly important to celebrate diversity and ensure that no one is excluded. Bias-based bullying undermines Canadian values and threatens our social fabric. It negatively affects the well-being of the victim and the perpetrator, as well as those who witness the bullying behaviour and the surrounding environment. It is harmful for individual children and their families, neighbourhoods, and schools, as well as society as a whole.[1]

This chapter explores bias-based bullying in more detail. We begin with a discussion of diversity in Canada in order to illustrate the context in which bias-based bullying occurs. Through this, we will see that an ever-growing number of Canadians identify with the social categories that are typically targets of bias. This is followed by an overview of research and discussion of the concept of intersectionality. We then turn to the complex problem of distinguishing bias-based bullying from harassment, and the associated legal implications. Finally, we discuss the critical role that adults can and should play in addressing biased, hurtful, and inappropriate behaviour among children and adolescents.

Canadian Context

Over the past two decades, the Canadian population has become significantly more diverse. We have seen growing immigrant and visible minority populations and ever-increasing linguistic and religious diversity in our society. According to the 2011 National Household Survey, almost one in five Canadians self-identify as a visible minority, an increase from approximately 16 percent recorded in 2006. The 2011 survey also recorded 6.8 million Canadian residents born outside the nation. This represents 21 percent of the total population, and includes those who are new to Canada as well as those who are long-term residents. Most of the 1.2 million individuals who arrived in Canada between 2006 and 2011 settled in a metropolitan area, most commonly in Toronto, Montreal, or Vancouver. According to the survey, of those born in Canada, 17 percent had at least one parent born elsewhere. This rich diversity strengthens our nation and should be celebrated. Unfortunately, however, this is not always the case. As we discuss below, bullying based on race, ethno-racial status, language, immigration status, and religion is a reality for some Canadian children and youth. This type of bullying is intimately connected to issues of racism and xenophobia, and can only be overcome if those larger issues are addressed.

The structure and role of the family vary depending on culture and context. Within the last 50 years, the structure of families has changed in Canada. The 2011 Census documented the increasing diversity of family structures, including a greater frequency of common-law couples, lone-parent families headed by men, and same-sex-parent families. While the number of married couples increased by 3 percent, the number of common-law families increased by almost 14 percent, and we saw an 8 percent increase in the number of lone-parent families. Between 2006 and 2011, the number of same-sex married couples in Canada nearly tripled. This reflects the first full five-year period for which same-sex marriage has been legal across the nation. For Canadian society to flourish, a widespread acceptance of this increased range of family structures is necessary. It comes as no surprise, however, that families deviating from the traditional nuclear structure face discrimination in our society. The bias against the lesbian, gay, bisexual, transgender, queer, and questioning (LGBTQ) community is well documented. Among young people, this bias is often expressed through homophobic and transphobic bullying.

Another social reality in Canada, as in all societies, is that a percentage of children face additional challenges. These include disabilities, which vary in severity and visibility. The 2006 Participation and Activity Limitation

Survey (PALS) identified approximately 125,000 children aged 5 to 14 living with a disability. This represents 4 percent of children in Canada. These disabilities include both physical and non-physical limitations, the most common being learning disabilities, chronic health conditions such as diabetes and asthma, speech conditions, autism, and attention deficit disorder. Of those children with a disability in Canada, 19 percent have a physical disability and 24 percent have a non-physical disability, while the majority (57 percent) have both physical and non-physical disabilities. Some of these children receive "special education," while others are integrated into mainstream classes or schools. Along with their peers, many of these children are connected to friends, acquaintances, and others in myriad ways, including via the cyber world. As we will discuss below, children with disabilities are particularly vulnerable to bullying. This is highly problematic and is clearly connected to the discrimination faced by people with disabilities in our society.[2]

Canada's diversity enriches the country in many ways. For instance, research suggests that increasing levels of ethnic diversity in schools are associated with decreased levels of victimization and loneliness, along with increased feelings of self-worth and school safety among students (Graham 2006; Juvonen, Nishina, & Graham 2006). Indeed, many Canadians embrace the great diversity in our nation and recognize that it only makes our country a better place. Importantly, however, we must remember that bias and discrimination are present in our society in both subtle and obvious ways, which results in marginalization for many of us.

An obvious example is the historic and contemporary colonization and discrimination experienced by First Nations, Métis, and Inuit peoples in Canada (Urban Aboriginal Peoples Study 2013; McCaskill 2012). The experience of Aboriginal peoples in Canada is distinguished from other Canadians in that they were not immigrants; they existed as self-sustaining, independent nations prior to colonization. Further, the Government of Canada specifically targeted Aboriginal peoples for assimilation through the Indian residential school regime and widespread disregard for treaty obligations. Counter to Canadian stereotypes, First Nations children on reserve receive fewer and more poorly funded education, health, and child welfare services than other Canadians, and many Aboriginal families lack basic amenities such as water, sewer, and electricity.

There have been countless unanswered calls to address the wide and unacceptable gap in basic human rights between First Nations, Métis, and Inuit people and non-Aboriginal people in Canada. Many of the contemporary disparities in socio-economic outcomes relate to historical and contemporary disadvantages such as residential schools and the ongoing inequities in services on reserves, but they are wrongly codified as personal or cultural deficits. This marginalization is both fuelled by and has contributed to stereotypes and bias that permeate the daily lives of Aboriginal peoples, including children.

With this context in mind, we should be concerned about the bullying faced by Aboriginal children and consider whether it is fuelled in part by bias. More research is needed to document the bullying involvement of Aboriginal young people. The results of a Canadian survey on racism conducted in 1993 suggest that the participating high school students generally supported all visible minority groups except for Aboriginal people. The results also indicate that there was considerable ambivalence among the participating students regarding Aboriginal peoples' rights and responsibilities. It is important that future research assess whether these negative attitudes are still present in Canadian schools, as this kind of bias likely contributes to a hostile school environment and bullying against Aboriginal young people.

In a more recent study on discrimination, anger, and aggression, researchers partnered with four US reservations and four Canadian First Nations reserves to recruit almost 700 adolescents and their caregivers to participate in interviews over several years. Researchers then conducted longitudinal analyses and found an association between perceived discrimination and later aggression, even when controlling for prior aggression, age, gender, income, and location. The study findings also suggest that anger may partially mediate the relationship between perceived discrimination and aggressive behaviour. That is, it may be that indigenous youth feel anger as a result of the discrimination they face, and this anger leads to an increased likelihood of aggressive behaviour. While not specifically focused on bullying, the findings from this study emphasize the detrimental effects of discrimination against indigenous children and youth in North America. These young people may be more likely to engage in bullying behaviour as a result of the discrimination they face, and perhaps they are also more likely to be victimized. There is clearly a pressing need to know more about bullying among indigenous young people in Canada in order to inform prevention and intervention efforts, and so that we can work toward eliminating discrimination and addressing its consequences.[3]

More subtle forms of bias and discrimination also exist in Canada. Consider the lingering marginalization of women, in spite of the significant progress we have made on gender issues in Canada. Girls grow up in an environment in which the implicit message is still that they are not equal with boys. Gender norms and ideals are behind this subtle discrimination. Girls grow up in a context in which their worth is dependent on superficial factors such as physical appearance, and any sign of strength or assertiveness is frowned upon as being too masculine. In this context, it is no surprise that women earn less than men, despite the closing gap between women and men in terms of labour force participation and educational attainment (Cool 2010). It is also no surprise that girls face sexualized and gendered bullying. For instance, a 15-year-old girl may be cyberbullied by a male classmate until she agrees to send a provocative photograph of herself to him. An 11-year-old girl may be called names and slurs such as "slut" and "whore" because she kissed a boy at summer camp. Female peers may call a 10-year-old girl "butch" because she speaks up in class and enjoys sports.

Many of us may face discrimination on the basis of a variety of other aspects of our diverse identities. Biases are taught to children from a very young age, sometimes explicitly and often implicitly. A father whose family has been in Canada for many generations might have a conversation at the dinner table about the newcomers who are getting hired at his workplace "fresh off the boat," and mention they are taking the jobs from "real" Canadians. A mother might comment on her son's friend, saying he always seemed "a bit light in the loafers," and warn her son not to have sleepovers with him. When consuming and interacting with media, children and youth may be predominantly exposed to images of white people, narratives about heterosexual relationships, and stories about people without disabilities or mental and physical health issues. When media include characters that are not white, heterosexual, able-bodied, and healthy, they are often poorly represented or laced with negative stereotypes. These messages can be internalized by young children and fuel bias-based bullying. We have seen that power imbalance is an important aspect of bullying dynamics. Bias and discrimination in our society automatically create inherent power imbalances among children from a very young age.

Bullying Based on Race, Ethnicity, or Religion

There is a small body of research on bullying based on race, ethnicity, immigration status, and religion in Canada. With support from CERIS, researchers Debra Pepler, Jennifer Connolly, and Wendy Craig studied the bullying experiences of minority and immigrant youth in Canada, focusing on students in grades 7 to 11 from five schools. The data were drawn from a larger longitudinal study on bullying and victimization. Students were asked to complete several questionnaires, including those focused on bullying, sexual harassment, dating, and relationships. Participants were also asked to nominate classmates who were most likely to bully and harass their peers. The findings suggest that ethnic minorities were not significantly more likely to self-identify as a bully or victim compared to students belonging to the ethnic majority. Likewise, immigration status (new to Canada compared to first- or second-generation Canadian) did not influence the likelihood that a young person would self-identify as a bully or victim. Even though there were general similarities in levels of bullying involvement based on ethnic and immigration status, almost one-fifth of all elementary and high school students involved in the study had been bullied by a student from another ethnic group because of their ethnicity. High school students who were not born in Canada experienced significantly more victimization related to their ethnic background. Those students who reported engaging in bullying based on ethnicity, as a bully or as a bully-victim, had the highest levels of externalizing behaviour problems. Interestingly, high school students of immigrant parents were more likely to report bullying others compared to second-generation students. The researchers hypothesize that this may be a result of the increasing frustration and hostility felt by these students due to their own experiences of victimization.

In a later analysis of data from the same longitudinal research project, Katherine McKenney along with Debra Pepler, Wendy Craig, and Jennifer Connolly further examined the bullying experiences of Canadian immigrant youth. They define ethnic bullying as any form of bullying that targets another person's ethnic background or cultural identity, which may include racial taunts and slurs, derogatory references to culturally specific traditions, and exclusion of certain peers based on their ethnic background. The results of this analysis suggest a stable relationship between ethnic victimization and maladjustment. In fact, ethnic victimization appears to have a distinct impact on adjustment, above and beyond general victimization. This specific form of victimization appears to contribute to anxiety, depression, withdrawal, aggression, and delinquent behaviours. The researchers hypothesize that this maladjustment may be a result of the self-blaming that can occur among victims. Young people who experience ethnic bullying may feel that the victimization is somehow their fault. These youth may feel particularly helpless because the aggression is related to their ethnicity, an uncontrollable and unalterable characteristic.

Although this longitudinal study did not explore the relationship between bias-based bullying and the wide variety of factors that may influence it, it is important to consider that everything from the geographic location of the school to the level of bias in a particular community can affect bullying. A key consideration is the environmental context in which bias-based bullying occurs. The ecological theoretical perspective can be particularly helpful when studying bias-based bullying precisely because it considers the broader context of the home, school, neighbourhood, community, and society. Larochette and colleagues studied racial bullying and victimization using Canadian data from the 2001/2002 Health Behaviour in School-Aged Children Survey (HBSC). These researchers used several theoretical perspectives to inform their analysis, including the ecological perspective and the theory of in-group bias. According to in-group bias theory, individuals form social groups based on shared characteristics such as race. Those who are outsiders are thought to be threatening in some way, fuelling feelings such as hatred and bias. The analysis examined racial bullying and victimization as the outcome variable of interest, with several demographic, school-related, and other variables used as predictors. Overall, approximately 4 percent of participating students reported racially bullying others and 4 percent reported experiencing racial victimization. Rates of general bullying and victimization were much higher. Several significant predictors of racial bullying were identified, including gender, age, race, and general victimization. Significant predictors of increased participation in racial bullying include being male, older, African-Canadian, and experiencing general victimization. Higher levels of school support were associated with lower levels of racial bullying, particularly in schools with high levels of teacher diversity. Not surprisingly, race was also associated with experiencing racial victimization. African-Canadian, East Asian-Canadian, Native-Canadian, and Southeast Asian-Canadian students were more likely to experience racial victimization.

Recently, Canadian researchers completed one of the first studies of bullying among indigenous children and youth in Canada. The sample included First Nations youth in grades five to eight living on reserve in Saskatchewan. Given the long history of cultural discrimination and marginalization that indigenous people in Canada have faced, it is important to study the bullying experiences of indigenous youth, as these experiences are likely connected to this tragic history. The results of the study revealed high rates of bullying among First Nations youth living on reserve. Over one-third had been physically victimized, while over half had been verbally bullied and 30 percent had been cyberbullied. In fact, prevalence rates were higher than those reported in other studies of the general population of Canadian young people. In line with other studies, reasons for bullying included appearance and body shape or weight. Contrary to other literature, however, this study found that youth who performed better in school and had a parent in a professional occupation were more likely to be victimized. More research is needed to fully understand these findings, although this seminal study provides crucial baseline information on the bullying experiences of indigenous children and youth. Future research should also examine bias-based bullying among indigenous children and youth living off reserve.[4]

In our study, we administered the "Safe School Questionnaire" (Pepler, Connolly, & Craig 1993, adapted from Olweus 1989) to 157 grade four and five students to obtain self-reports of involvement in bullying. We also obtained the perspectives of their parents and educators.[5] One question asked respondents to list the reasons they were bullied. Race was listed by 16 percent of respondents, and religion was listed by 12 percent. A smaller proportion of students reported being bullied up to several times per week for reasons of race (6 percent) or religion (2 percent). This study was conducted in a large urban centre in Canada, with the participating schools being diverse in terms of family income and composition as well as the immigration status of students. Two of the schools were attended by students from primarily low-income families, often headed by a single parent. Many of the families of students in these schools were new to the country. The other two schools that participated had students living in higher-income families, often headed by two parents with high education levels. Although the sample was diverse, the findings of this study are representative of the particular metropolitan area in which the study was conducted and may not be representative of other locations, such as rural areas.

Researchers in other countries have studied bullying related to race, ethnicity, and religion, with mixed results. While some studies suggest minority students are more likely to experience victimization, others have found that bullying based on race, ethnicity, and religion is relatively uncommon compared to other forms of bullying. Study findings can be challenging to muddle through, and much of the inconsistency in results may be due to differences in methodologies used across studies, sample characteristics, and importantly, the definitions used. Some young people may not feel their experiences fit into the definition of "bias-based bullying" offered by researchers, even though they may have experienced aggression or abuse based on their race, ethnicity, and/or religion.[6]

Gender

Children should be able to grow up without facing discrimination based on gender or sexuality. Gendered bullying and sexual harassment represent two widespread forms of aggressive behaviour, which are often difficult to untangle. Sexual harassment is considered a form of discrimination and is prohibited by law. Gendered and sexualized bullying are closely connected to sexual harassment, and include any form of bullying that is based on one's gender or sexuality, as well as any bullying rooted in misogyny and patriarchy.

Sexual harassment may be considered bullying if it has the elements we typically consider to constitute bullying behaviour. This form of harassment is certainly aggressive and it is likely intentional. It may or may not happen repeatedly, and a power imbalance may be present. It may happen directly or indirectly, and it may occur face-to-face or in the cyber world. Some scholars have argued that distinguishing between sexual harassment and sexual bullying is unproductive, because even if a specific aggressive incident does not meet the traditional bullying criteria, any sexualized aggression among children and youth fosters a climate in which bullying based on gender and sexuality is supported.

It has been suggested that gendered discrimination is so pervasive in North America and elsewhere around the world that by simply attending school every day, girls are at risk of sexual harassment. In other words, they are subject to unwanted sexual attention that may include a continuum of behaviours ranging from very mild (and given the frequency of these behaviours, they may in fact be considered "normal") to very severe, even violent. Much of this harassment may represent bullying as we traditionally have defined it. There is compelling evidence that sexualized aggression is pervasive from kindergarten through high school. Girls are most often targeted, but boys can also experience such bullying based on norms about masculinity. Studies show that on the whole, girls experience more frequent, physical, and severe sexual harassment than do boys, although boys more commonly face homophobic slurs. Sexualized aggression often occurs in such public locations as the classroom or the hallway, in view of teachers and other adults as well as students. Even when young people seek help, they may not receive it. Some report that teachers fail to take their distress seriously, doing little to intervene.[7]

This pattern emerged in our study of grade four and five students (described above) and their parents and teachers. Several of these participants (including students, parents, and teachers) reported that a number of adults witnessed—but did not respond to—incidents of sexual bullying among peers. Nor, according to participant reports, did the adults respond to the victimized student's apparent or expressed upset. These adults had characterized such incidents as a "normal part of development." For example, a girl was distressed because a boy kept trying "to touch her chest," so she relayed the situation to her mother. In recounting the incident to the researcher, this girl's mother defined the boy's actions in benign, nonthreatening language: his behaviour, according to the mother, only revealed that the boy "liked her." No surprise that the girl was further distressed by her mother's failure to help, given the mother's perception that the behaviour was "a normal part of growing up." The mother certainly did not label the behaviour as bullying or sexual harassment. In another example, a teacher excused bullying behaviour against a girl who she described as "adorable," attributing the behaviour to schoolboys' crushes. A group of boys would frequently call this girl names and take her possessions in order to make her attempt to retrieve them. The teacher did not intervene. She reported that it never "crossed her mind" that the girl might feel threatened and upset, adding, "It is hard at this age to say whether they want to hurt her when she is so adorable. Boys say things to get her attention and show off, like a courting thing." While the content of this bullying was not sexualized, the lack of response on behalf of the teacher reflected patriarchal norms that privileged the boys' apparent romantic interests over the girl's right to feel safe and live free of victimization. In both of the examples, the mother and teacher were concerned and wanted to be helpful, but were unable to recognize the negative impact of the bullying on the girls, despite each girl's indication of being distressed. Parents, teachers, and school administrators would benefit from education on understanding and identifying incidents of gendered and sexualized bullying.[8]

Sexual Minorities

Homophobic bullying is pervasive, insidious, and starts early. It has been documented in schools as well as other settings, such as group homes and foster homes (Mallon 2001; O'Brien 1994; Solomon & Russel 2004). LGBTQ youth are significantly more likely to experience verbal, physical, and sexual harassment, as well as prejudice and discrimination in school and the community. The same is true of young people who have sexual minority parents. US studies suggest that up to 84 percent of sexual minority youth experience verbal harassment and one-quarter experience physical harassment. It comes as no surprise that these negative experiences can result in long-term consequences for the mental and physical health of sexual minority youth. But bullying based on sexual minority status is not only harmful to LGBTQ youth; it can have extremely negative consequences for all children and youth.

Elizabeth Saewyc, a Canadian researcher, conducted a comprehensive literature review and noted that studies from across North America, the United Kingdom, and other parts of the world point to a strong and consistent pattern: LGBQ students report more harassment, bullying, and physical assaults at school compared with heterosexual peers. Together with colleagues, Saewyc also led several studies on the health and lives of lesbian, gay, and bisexual youth in schools in British Columbia. Youth in grades 7 to 12 were surveyed in 1992, 1998, and 2003 as part of the BC Adolescent Health Survey. According to the 2003 survey, sexual minority youth are generally more likely to report verbal harassment at school, along with experiences of being purposefully excluded and physically assaulted either at school or on their way to and from school. Perhaps as a result of these experiences, sexual minority youth tended to feel less safe at school. The findings also suggest that discrimination against gay males and bisexual youth has increased over time from 1992 to 2003. Many life experiences and health issues were similar for lesbian, gay, and bisexual youth regardless of whether they lived in an urban centre, a rural set-ting, or a small town, including experiences of discrimination. Lesbian, gay, and bisexual teens living in rural areas, however, were more likely to report that they had been in contact with a stranger on the Internet who made them feel unsafe.[9]

Peer victimization based on sexual orientation is not limited to high school. It has been identified across all school levels, including elemen-tary and university settings. Researcher Daniel Chesir-Teran argues that schools can support or suppress sexual minority identities to varying degrees, depending on the levels of heterosexism present. Whereas the concept of homophobia implies a person-centred emotional reaction to homosexuality, heterosexism refers to the systemic process which results in the privileging of heterosexuality relative to homosexuality. The re-sult of heterosexism is essentially that heterosexuality is believed to be normal, ideal, and better than every other kind of sexuality. Along with other scholars, Chesir-Teran puts forth that students will be at greater risk for poor outcomes when they attend schools characterized by high levels of heterosexism. Heterosexism may manifest in schools in several ways. Perhaps sex education classes only focus on content applicable to opposite-sex relationships, or posters seen around school only feature heterosexual couples. Or, it may be that there are no specific school pol-icies against discrimination and harassment on the basis of sexuality, or alternatively no books on LGBTQ issues in the library. Non-heterosexual families may never be discussed in classes, or perhaps the achievements of LGBTQ authors and historical figures are not discussed. Heterosexism is definitely embodied in the language used in schools, beginning at a very early age. Research suggests that homophobic comments and labels are often used in schools and are directed toward individuals regardless of their sexual orientation. This begins in elementary school with comments such as "that's so gay." These and other seemingly small manifestations of heterosexism contribute to the culture of a given school and can be highly influential in either perpetuating or reducing victimization of LGBTQ students.[10]

Disabilities

Research has shown that students with disabilities and "special education" needs are at substantially greater risk of peer victimization, as are students with chronic medical conditions.[11] A recent Canadian study found that young people with cerebral palsy frequently experience social exclusion and isolation from their peers at school, and also face name-calling, derogatory comments, and less frequently, even physical victimization. In our research, slightly less than one-third of all the respondents reported being bullied as a result of their learning difficulties. Another Canadian study found that many children with autism spectrum disorder experience chronic bullying, sometimes even several kinds of bullying at a time (physical, verbal, and cyber). In this study, victimized children sometimes displayed anxiety, hyperactivity, self-injurious and stereotypic behaviours, and over-sensitivity, and they had more communication difficulties and fewer school-based friendships. It is unclear whether these issues were a result of bullying, or factors that contributed to their increased risk of bullying. More research is needed on bullying among children and youth with disabilities in Canada, as well as on ways to reduce bias and discrimination against all people with disabilities in our nation and abroad.[12]

Intersectionalities

Intersectionality refers to "particular forms of intersecting oppressions." This might include "intersections of race and gender, or of sexuality and nation. Intersectional paradigms remind us that oppression cannot be reduced to one fundamental type and that all oppressions work together in producing injustice" (Collins 2000, 18). An intersectional approach focuses attention on the interactive relationships among the various aspects of social identity, including, for example, race/ethnicity, gender, sexual orientation, ability, and newcomer/citizenship status. For instance, a 14-year-old girl may be bullied based on newcomer status, having recently immigrated to Canada from Bangladesh. At the same time, the girl may be bullied because of her poor language skills and her learning difficulties, both of which might be connected to her newcomer status. She may also face taunting and mocking about the way she dresses. For this particular young girl, her experiences of victimization are all connected and all must be addressed. We must attend to the context to determine why young people might be biased against newcomers, girls and women, and children with different abilities in this way. Is diversity celebrated in her school? Are students exposed to a wide variety of ideas and individuals? Are children valued and respected regardless of their abilities? What values and norms are communicated to the children at school and in the community? Addressing all aspects of this girl's experience will be much more beneficial than focusing on any of her singular experiences of oppression based on her newcomer status, gender, and abilities.

Intersectionality does not imply an additive approach to understanding victimization. That is, a 14-year-old African-Canadian girl is not at risk for double bullying, per se, because of her race and gender. Rather, she may be at risk for racialized sexual bullying. This means she may experience a particular form of sexual bullying based on her racial background. Boys in her class might post sexually degrading lyrics from a popular song by an African-Canadian artist to her social media page, asking if she is like the girls in the song. In another example, a 17-year-old girl who identifies as a lesbian might face constant sexual taunts from the boys in school. Her tormenters might grab at her sexually and tell her she will not be a "lesbo" anymore if she has sex with them, or ask her to kiss her girlfriend in front of them as a "turn-on." Importantly, with an intersectional approach, no one single factor is privileged as the explanation for abuse or oppression, and a multi-faceted response is promoted.[13]

"Bias-Based Bullying" and/or "Harassment"

We have seen how all forms of bullying can and do have detrimental effects on young people. It is important to be clear about unacceptable behaviours, and labelling certain behaviours as bullying gives a clear message. Paradoxically, giving certain behaviours the label of "bullying" can minimize their gravity. Several authors worry that including bias-based bullying within the broader bullying category may conceal underlying motivations and minimize the gravity of the bias and its enactment (Greene 2006; Stein 2003). Within the inclusive bullying label, certain actions may be disregarded. These could include assaults, hate crimes, and discrimination due to disability, gender, sexual orientation, religion, and race. Labelling such behaviours as bullying can result in overlooking the human or civil rights violations of the students who are victimized by virtue of their membership in a particular group.

Take, for instance, the following example. A group of popular students at a high school is primarily comprised of adolescent boys who identify as white or Asian. The school is located in an affluent suburban area in Ontario. Another student, John, is a visible minority, identifying as African-Canadian. The popular boys begin to harass him when they encounter him in the hallways, using racialized taunts and some pushing. Other students witness these incidents, but given the boys' popularity, these witnesses fail to intervene. This culminates in an incident in which one of the boys spits on John and shouts a racial slur. Is this a case of bullying or bias-based bullying? Is it an assault motivated by hate? If we label this instance "bias-based bullying," does it seem less severe and less related to racial discrimination than if we label it a "hate crime"? It is difficult to determine how to label this incident and how to respond. Looking at the incident through the lens of human rights helps us unpack these complicated questions.

Bias-Based Bullying, the Rights of Children and Youth, and Legal Responses

What happened to John is a human rights violation, regardless of the label. Naming the incident (correctly) as a violation of his rights, however, clarifies that it requires a definitive response on the part of the school board, as a matter of protecting John's rights under Canadian and international law.

According to the Canadian Charter of Rights and Freedoms, every individual has the right to equal protection regardless of race, national or ethnic origin, colour, religion, sex, age, or mental or physical disability.[14] Bias-based bullying and other forms of discriminatory harassment are violations of human rights. These rights are protected in several ways, including through the United Nations Convention on the Rights of the Child (UNCRC), the Canadian Human Rights Act, the Criminal Code, and school sanctions.

The UNCRC is the first legally binding international instrument to incorporate a wide range of human rights, including civil, cultural, economic, political, and social rights. It was developed to protect young people, who often need special care and protection that adults do not. This legal instrument also outlines the basic human rights of children everywhere, including the right to be protected from abuse and exploitation. Canada has agreed to undertake the obligations of the convention, which means that our federal government has committed to protecting and to ensuring children's rights, including through prevention and intervention in instances of bias-based bullying (UNICEF 2013b). Canada fulfills this obligation by enforcing the Canadian Human Rights Act to protect children.

The *Canadian Human Rights Act* outlines every Canadian's right to live without discrimination based on race, national or ethnic origin, colour, religion, age, sex, sexual orientation, marital status, family status, disability, or conviction for an offence for which a pardon has been granted or a record suspension has been ordered. The Canadian Human Rights Commission accepts harassment complaints, defining harassment as a form of discrimination that involves any unwanted physical or verbal behaviour that offends or humiliates the victim. In addition to this national act, every province and territory has legislation to prohibit discrimination.[15]

If an incident of bias-based bullying represents criminal behaviour according to the Canadian *Criminal Code*, the incident may be considered a hate crime. Hate crimes are generally recognized within Canada, the United States, and the United Kingdom as crimes perpetrated against a person due to actual or perceived demographic factors, with differences in definition and applicable legal codes. In Canada, "hate crime" is a broad term that applies both to specific Criminal Code offences (i.e., advocating genocide, public incitement of hatred, willful promotion of hatred, and mischief in relation to religious property) and to any Criminal Code offence motivated by hatred toward a particular group based on race, national or ethnic origin, language, colour, religion, sex, age, mental or physical disability, sexual orientation, or any other similar characteristic of an individual or group. For instance, criminal harassment, assault, or defamatory libel may all be considered hate crimes if these actions are motivated by hatred toward a particular group.

According to a report by Statistics Canada, Canadian police services reported 1,401 hate crimes in 2010, which is likely a low estimate given that many crimes go unreported. Hate crimes were most commonly motivated by race, ethnicity, religion, or sexual orientation in Canada in 2010, with black people being the most commonly targeted racial group and Jewish people the most commonly targeted religious group. According to Statistics Canada, hate crimes targeting sexual minorities, such as those individuals identifying as gay or lesbian, were more likely to be violent and to result in physical injury to victims. This report revealed that young people between the ages of 12 and 17 were most commonly accused of perpetrating hate crimes, with rates peaking at age 16. Victims of hate crimes tended to be slightly older, with the highest rates reported for those who were 22 years old (Dowden & Brennan 2012).

In some cases, legal responses to bias-based bullying may be appropriate under Canadian human rights and criminal legislation. In other cases, *school responses* might be most appropriate. Chapter 2 described how school sanctions such as suspension and expulsion may be applied in cases of bias-based bullying. School administrators are responsible for creating an environment that offers equal opportunities for children to learn without fear, and must rectify situations in which such an environment is jeopardized. If school authorities fail to address bias-based bullying, the resulting dangerous environment is not acceptable by law. In North Vancouver School District No. 44 v. Jubran,[16] a British Columbia teen successfully sued the school board under British Columbia's Human Rights Act after suffering years of homophobic bullying that negatively affected his educational experience—even though he was not gay and his tormentors knew it.

American legal responses to bullying vary slightly from the Canadian approach. Federal law in the United States protects citizens against discrimination in various contexts, such as employment, education, and access to government services, on the basis of specified grounds such as race and gender. John—the African-Canadian boy described above who was continuously subject to racialized harassment in school—would be protected by federal civil rights laws if the same acts took place in the United States. All states have similar counterpart laws but the specific grounds vary, reflecting local values. For instance, unlike Canada, only a minority of states prohibits discrimination on the grounds of sexual orientation. Further, whereas hate speech is prohibited under the Canadian Criminal Code ("wilful promotion of hatred"), the United States has no "hate speech" prohibition because any such restriction on speech would be unconstitutional under the First Amendment to the United States Constitution, which is applicable to American children as well as to adults. Likewise, school sanctions against bullying are limited by the First Amendment.

Role of Adults in Responding to Bias-Based Bullying

Above and beyond the many detrimental effects of victimization on students' emotional, social, academic, and physical functioning, bias-based bullying may cause young people to hide the identities for which they are victimized, such as religious affiliation, sexual orientation, or ethnicity. This bullying is both a reflection of and a contributor to a toxic environment that fosters victimization. It is crucial that both individual incidents and the larger environmental context are addressed.[17]

The first step in responding to bias-based bullying is recognizing that it is taking place. We must pay more attention to the specific content of aggressive behaviours among children and adolescents in order to pick up on homophobic, sexist, racist, ableist, and other discriminatory undertones. We must also pay attention to the everyday language that contributes to discrimination on a broader level. For instance, language that demeans female behaviours (e.g., "quit acting like a girl") is common from kindergarten through high school. Degrading language of all varieties may reflect prejudice toward particular groups that is sanctioned within society—or, alternatively, this language may reflect entrenched habits with no thought to or recognition of the meaning or impact. In either case, it must be identified and addressed.[18]

Upon witnessing instances of bias and discrimination among children and youth, adults must not remain silent. Aside from the legal issues this raises, young people might interpret this silence as an expression of norms and values that condone such behaviours. Inaction is not simply a lost opportunity; it represents a stance that may result in more harm because it has enabled discrimination to become an acceptable mode of interaction. Further, if a young person witnesses an adult ignoring an act of discrimination it is unlikely that he or she will disclose experiences of victimization in the future. Marginalized children and youth might not feel comfortable seeking help with bullying, particularly if it appears that adults hold biases.

LGBTQ youth or those with "invisible" disabilities may not want to tell adults about their victimization experiences because this might "out" them. In order to facilitate disclosure, children and youth must feel safe and comfortable approaching adults and must feel all aspects of their identities will be accepted.

Adults can uncover bias-based bullying even in the absence of reports by the victimized young people. Adults should ask questions and be alert to signs such as a child's greater reluctance to attend school, worsening self-esteem, or unexplained damage to his or her possessions. When youth do tell, adults must respond in a way that is validating and that encourages children to keep talking. Many students do overcome their reluctance to ask for help, and often find interventions by parents, teachers, and peers effective (Hunter, Boyle, & Warden 2004).

An intersectional approach to bias-based bullying is most helpful, as it focuses on the youth as a "whole person." This perspective validates the importance of all dimensions of the young person, including for example his or her race, gender, sexual orientation, and ability. By recognizing and responding to multiple oppressions at the same time, the youth is not required to leave out part of his or her experience or identity. Take, for instance, the example discussed above of the 17-year-old girl who faced sexualized homophobic bullying. In this case, we must ensure that in addressing the situation, we validate her experience as both a lesbian who has faced homophobic bullying and a girl who has faced sexualized bullying. We must also ensure that the perpetrators are held accountable for both the homophobic and sexualized aspects of the bullying. We should not simply punish the boys without actually working toward combatting both homophobia and gender inequality at the school level.

It is not enough to label discriminatory behaviours as bullying. The underlying biases must not be minimized; they need to be brought into the open, named for what they are, and have consequences attached. A father might decide to have a conversation with his son about why calling a friend's shirt "gay" is hurtful. A teacher might organize a class-wide discussion about why it is wrong to use judgmental and hurtful language to describe a classmate who frequently acts problematically. Even small actions by a teacher—forbidding disparaging comments about students with disabilities, for example, or discussing LGBTQ issues in class—can communicate acceptance to youth. This provides support, and may help offset negative experiences. It is also important for teachers and administrators to reflect on the school environment as a whole and identify areas in which discrimination might exist at the institutional level. When bias exists at the school level, it is more likely that bias-based bullying will occur among individual children. This bias may be subtle and difficult to detect, partly because it is so often normalized. When schools do take a stance against discrimination, however, hate-motived bullying decreases (Lindsay & McPherson 2012; Taylor & Peter 2011).

Before concluding, it is worth returning to the example of John. How might we respond if faced with this situation? An important first step would be to attend to John's immediate distress. He may need to see a counsellor or mental health professional. After addressing any more urgent needs, we may consider asking John his preferences for how to respond to the perpetrators. John may desire a punitive response, or alternatively may not want any adult intervention out of fear that the situation might deteriorate. It might also be beneficial to consult with John's family to determine their preferred response. It would be important to balance the wishes of John and his family with the understanding that it is not an option to have no response. That is, even if it were John's preference to ignore the situation, the responsible adults in his life should nevertheless take action to ensure that the perpetrators face meaningful consequences for the incident and to convey the message that bias, harassment, discrimination, and bullying are unacceptable. But this intervention would ideally be sensitive to John's concerns, and also avoid placing him at greater risk for victimization. John and his family may consider filing a harassment complaint to the Canadian Human Rights Commission or a police report for a hate crime. In any case, a restorative justice approach might be beneficial in this situation. Discussed in more detail in Chapter 6, restorative justice allows victims to face the individuals who caused them distress and express how and why their actions were harmful. In this way, John and his perpetrators could together determine how to move forward in a constructive and healing fashion. School administrators should also consider implementing programs and policies to increase acceptance of racial and ethnic diversity, and to raise awareness of the harmful impact of racism. Of utmost importance, the teachers and administrators at John's school must ensure that the incident is taken seriously and not minimized, normalized, or tolerated.

Concluding Comments

Environments that either actively or passively support a hostile milieu for any population of students can foster bias-based bullying and impede the success of any anti-bullying efforts (Murdock & Bolch 2005). Adults must attend to the psychological and social effects of bias-based bullying. They must also be fully aware of the victim's human rights, and of their duty to protect those rights. Marginalization and prejudice must be addressed at all levels—individual, family, school, community, and societal—in order to combat this pervasive and destructive behaviour.

Chapter 4

Bullying Among Friends and Siblings

Introduction

Relationships with peers and friends are hugely important to young people, and the same is generally true of siblings, although of course the nature of these relationships is different. Chapters 1 through 3 focused on introducing the problem of bullying, discussing the different mediums through which it can occur, and describing the various forms it can take. In this chapter, we consider the relationships in which bullying occurs. Up to this point, we have described bullying occurring in the peer context. Importantly, however, all the forms of bullying that we discussed can occur in the context of specific relationships. This chapter considers bullying that occurs within friendships and sibling relationships, and offers strategies for response. The particular relational context in which bullying occurs adds a layer of complexity that can be difficult to understand. However, adults must evaluate the relational dynamics as fully as possible in order to determine how best to respond.[1]

Bullying Among Friends

Positive relationships with friends offer enormous benefits to young people, even helping to protect against adversity. Qualities such as mutual affection, trust, sharing, and communication characterize healthy, high-quality friendships. Such relationships can teach children important lessons that will influence their future interactions with friends, romantic partners, family members, co-workers, and others. Importantly, healthy friendships in elementary, middle, and high school teach lifelong skills in conflict resolution. Friendships, however, are not always healthy and may involve manipulation, exclusion, power, and control. Unhealthy early relationships can set the stage for future relationship problems.[2]

We discussed above how scholars have recently moved toward understanding bullying as a relationship problem. When children bully, it is evidence that they have difficulty relating to others. They may have trouble with specific situations or general problems in the way they relate. Children involved in bullying, as a bully or victim, often struggle to form and maintain healthy, high-quality friendships. Both quality and quantity matter when it comes to relationships.

Young people may struggle with relating for a variety of reasons. A child with a learning disability, for example, might have trouble making friends at school because he is so often frustrated by his difficulty grasping certain concepts in class. Hot-tempered and irritable, he might be perceived as abrasive and annoying by the other children and may experience considerable rejection and bullying by peers. This child may bully others as a way of releasing his anger and deflecting attention from his learning problems and his own victimization. Similarly, a teen whose first language is not English may find it daunting to make friends at her new school. Shy and desperate for friends, this teen may be vulnerable to victimization by peers and newfound acquaintances. She may tolerate unbalanced or aggressive friendships for fear of losing these relationships. In both situations, these young people are faced with difficulties in developing high-quality friendships, which may be connected to their continued involvement in bullying.

Strategies for Responding to Bullying Among Friends

In order to respond to bullying among friends, adults must first be aware that this behaviour is occurring. It can be particularly challenging, however, for adults to identify bullying within friendships. By virtue of the friendship itself, the bullying dynamics may be more difficult to discern. Adults may be uncertain whether the behaviour constitutes bullying or reflects "normal" conflict. Moreover, we know it is very difficult for a victimized child to disclose bullying generally. Disclosure becomes even more challenging when the aggressor is a friend. Despite the victimization, the child might still feel a sense of closeness to the aggressor, may not even identify the behaviour as bullying, and might attribute any difficulties to him or herself. Telling an adult about a friend can feel like a betrayal, and the perceived risk of losing the friend might outweigh any benefit of turning to an adult for help.

Given that many children have difficulty telling a parent or teacher about bullying by friends, it is important for adults to be aware of children's friendships and alert to problematic patterns. Adults must first and foremost have a solid understanding of what constitutes healthy relationships in order to identify unhealthy patterns. Even with keen awareness, however, it can be difficult to distinguish bullying from practical jokes, good-natured teasing, and the inevitable conflict that arises in all relationships. An incident that may seem like a "mean" or cruel joke to outsiders may be experienced as "just fun" or "drama"[3] among friends, and in contrast, a situation that seems benign to adults might be experienced as hurtful or as bullying by the child or youth. Particularly with relational aggression, bullying among friends is often subtle and challenging to detect.

When trying to understand the relationship dynamics among children and teens, and intervening in problematic situations, it may be helpful to recall definitions of bullying. Is a young person intentionally behaving aggressively toward a friend? Does this behaviour occur repeatedly? Does one child seem to generally have more power than another, for any number of reasons? Upon reflection, the dynamics among friends may become clear, and this may make it easier to identify problematic patterns such as bullying. Importantly, the dynamics of bullying among friends may differ from other bullying situations among peers. In some cases, the aggression might be reciprocal and the power imbalance might shift back and forth in the relationship, adding to the confusion and to the uncertainty regarding intervention. We must carefully appraise the qualities within a given relationship. For example, it is important to consider whether the friendship appears voluntary and equal; whether one child seems to "need" the friendship at all costs; and whether there are problems such as aggression, an entrenched power imbalance, or high levels of conflict. Although in some situations this might be a straightforward matter, in others it can be extremely complex. Once problematic patterns are identified, it is critical for parents and teachers to open lines of communication with all children involved.

If a child does choose to disclose an incident of bullying, the dilemma he or she faces should be acknowledged. Adults must not dismiss the friendship, insisting that the aggressor is "not really a friend," or advise "finding other friends." This may put the child in a bind; he or she may feel ill-prepared for such advice, which might inhibit future disclosure. More helpful may be to show empathy for the situation while at the same time helping the child find strategic solutions. It may also be important to encourage the child to grasp the fact that while conflict in relationships is normal, healthy relationships do not cause chronic distress or confusion. An adult can encourage the child to become friends with others who treat them with respect and care; this may involve the adult actively structuring activities with other peers.

The child or youth needs to feel understood and comfortable moving forward at his or her own pace. If a young person is not ready to end the friendship or address concerns with the friend, adults must balance a respect for this decision with the reality that ignoring a harmful situation is also not a solution. A fine balance must be struck between listening and validating the experiences of young people and ensuring that they understand that the situation must improve. Clearly, addressing bullying among friends is difficult for both children and adults alike.

It is important to remember that some children may not even realize they are being bullied. If an adult identifies an unhealthy relationship, it is best to take advantage of the opportunity to teach children about positive, trusting, and mutually beneficial relationships. This can also be an opportunity to teach better communication and conflict-resolution skills, and to clarify the difference between normal conflict and bullying. Children generally need help understanding what constitutes bullying in order to be able to recognize when it is happening in their friendships and other relationships. A teenager who coerces a friend may not realize why this is wrong. A child who is "teased" by his friends for being overweight may not see this as bullying even though it is ongoing and highly upsetting. A girl who is often told to "go away" by her two best friends might think they are "just joking" or playing, although this behaviour hurts and confuses her. In a particularly worrying pattern, she might even feel her friends act this way because she is "irritating," or that there is some reason which justifies such behaviour. By learning about healthy relationships and about how to identify problematic behaviour, children and adolescents might be better able to recognize signs of bullying, rather than dismissing the behaviours.

Scaffolding and social architecture

Debra Pepler has applied the concept of scaffolding[4] to bullying interventions. The metaphor of scaffolding "refers to the process of anticipation and directed instruction to provide dynamic supports for learning so that children can perform above their normal levels. As children become increasingly skilled, the scaffolds can be gradually dismantled, only to be set up again to support the next developmental stretch" (Pepler 2006, 17). In order to put scaffolding into action, adults must consider what types of skills and capacities are required for children to shift out of roles such as bully and victim and into healthy relationships. Adults must contemplate what children who bully need in terms of relationship skills. Examples of questions to ask include: Does a particular child lack empathy or emotional regulation? Does he or she have poor social skills? Once areas of need are identified, targeted interventions can be applied. Much of the time, however, scaffolding occurs informally in daily life at home, at school, and in the community. For this reason, it is important that open and mutual communication occur among the adults in a child's life, such as parents, teachers, counsellors, and others who deliver targeted interventions. This communication can also help adults anticipate children's needs. For instance, a counsellor may identify that a particular child who bullies does not have the social or cognitive skills to resist peer pressure. This should be communicated to all adults involved in this child's life so that they can better know when he or she will have problems, and when to provide support at appropriate times; such support should of course be sensitive to all the children involved. The concept of scaffolding can be applied not only to children who bully and are victimized, but also to bystanders.

Pepler describes the concept of social architecture as the process of structuring children's peer groups to promote positive experiences and prevent negative interactions. This can take place by separating the bully and victim to help develop better relationship skills for both. Alternatively, it can also occur by placing victimized children in a positive peer group. In such a situation, for instance, a teacher may assign children to groups for activities rather than allowing children to choose their own groups. Finally, promoting a positive, respectful, and supportive climate at home, school, and in the community will go a long way toward structuring children's lives to promote positive peer experiences. To utilize social architecture on an ongoing basis, it is advisable for adults to remain alert and active in their efforts to promote healthy relationships among children. Parents, teachers, and other adults may require assistance and scaffolding themselves in order to learn how to effectively use scaffolding and social architecture to assist children, as often it is not clear what they should do.

Nature of the interventions

Education about relationships starts at home and continues at school. This can take place directly, through discussions about healthy relationships; and it can also take place indirectly, through observation. Young people constantly watch and learn about relationships from the adults around them. Lessons about relating to others come in many forms, from witnessing parents resolve arguments to teachers interacting with students. Adults who treat others with respect and care are modelling this behaviour to the children around them.

Education about policies will be sufficient for many children. Others, however, will require more targeted interventions. Such interventions may involve teaching conflict-management skills, improving self-esteem to decrease a child's vulnerability to victimization, or teaching a child to manage his or her anger more adaptively. Some children may already have significant problems and may require individual or family counselling, or a support group. It is critical to enhance children's skills in forming and maintaining relationships, including conflict management. This applies to both children who bully and those who are victimized (Asher, Parker, & Walker 1996).

Myths and facts

There are many stereotypes associated with bullying. Most people can conjure up a mental image of the stereotypical bully: the aggressive boy, who has a group of other more or less "cool kids" hanging around him, who preys on the "nerdy" boys; or the popular but manipulative pretty girl, who maintains her position on the social ladder with a certain ruthlessness, while other girls vying to be in her circle push out others through bullying. These stereotypes are limiting, however, and may prevent adults from identifying instances of bullying among friends and responding appropriately. These myths should be debunked. For example, it is a common belief that friendships in which children are bullied are not "real" or "true" friendships. In fact, it is the child's perception of the friendship that matters. If the child believes the bully is a friend, the friendship is real to him or her; adults must understand this if they want to help. Another common myth is that children involved in bullying with friends must have low self-esteem and lack self-confidence, and that they must struggle with overall adjustment. In reality, many children involved in bullying among friends and peers are well-adjusted and good students, even though bullying involvement places children at risk for problems with mental health and academics. Indeed, the impact of bullying is influenced by various risk and protective factors in a child's life. Finally, many believe that children who bully their friends do not have social skills. Rather, some children who bully—for example, in relational bullying—possess rather sophisticated social skills. These skills can actually help children manipulate and victimize others, including friends.

Bullying Among Friends: Case Examples

Case Example 1

Phillip is a bright fifteen-year-old boy in the gifted program. Frustrated that he was labelled by peers he admired as a "brainer" and "geek," Phillip joined a recreational hockey league. He had played for several years when younger, but stopped because his parents could no longer afford it. Now a teenager, Phillip promised his parents he would find a part-time job to help pay for the cost of hockey. Soon, he was playing weekly on a local team with Derek, a boy from school. The other team members attended different schools. Derek was friendly, much to Phillip's surprise, and the two boys had a few good laughs at the first

continued

practice. The following week at school, Phillip saw Derek sitting with a group of popular boys during the lunch hour, and approached the table hoping to join them. Derek stared blankly at him, however, and mumbled "hi" in a barely audible voice, then ignored him. Confused and hurt, Phillip muttered and walked off to eat with his friends in the gifted program. At the next hockey practice, Derek was friendly again, even suggesting they play video games on the weekend. Over the next several months, Derek and Phillip grew closer as friends, but only outside of school hours. Upon seeing Phillip at school, Derek would ignore him completely or, at times, even laugh when some of his popular friends mocked Phillip. Initially very distressed, Phillip came to "accept" that this was "just the way it is." He did not want to risk losing the times he spent with Derek outside of school, which he valued greatly, and therefore remained silent about his friend's hurtful behaviour and did not confront Derek.

Like Phillip, other young people are bullied by friends. In some situations, it is questionable whether the youth who is doing the bullying considers the victim a friend, even though the victim may believe in the friendship. In other cases, youth may value a friendship that involves bullying. In this example, it appears that Derek enjoyed the time he spent with Phillip, although he ostracized Phillip when he was with his "popular" friends. This behaviour both confused and hurt Phillip. Although we don't know the motivation behind Derek's incongruent behaviour, we can speculate that he may not have wanted his popular friends to learn about his relationship with Phillip. Along with his friends, Derek's actions can be considered bullying.

Even if adults were aware of this situation, it would be challenging for them to understand and know how to intervene. The consequences of not intervening, however, can be grave. The dynamics of this relationship are teaching both boys harmful lessons they each may carry into their adult years. Phillip is learning that he does not deserve to be treated with respect and kindness in his relationships, and that he may need to tolerate certain kinds of behaviours such as exclusion in order to maintain valued relationships. He is learning not to confront such problematic behaviour, as doing so could put the relationship at risk. His self-esteem is likely becoming even lower, and on some level he may be suppressing feelings of betrayal and anger because of Derek's duplicitous behaviour. We must not forget Derek. He is learning that it is acceptable to be inconsistent in his treatment of "friends" or others he cares about; and he is finding out that when he acts disrespectfully he will not be challenged and therefore that there is no consequence to such behaviour.

How might an adult notice this problematic but subtle pattern? It might not ever be noticed. Or perhaps school staff might notice the group treating

Phillip in a demeaning way, and in following up, the boys' outside friendship may emerge. Although it is unlikely Phillip will tell an adult, his parents may begin to see changes in him if he becomes increasingly upset.

How should an adult respond? First and foremost, adults must recognize the complexity of the situation because of the boys' friendship. This necessitates a balanced response; this is not an easy matter to settle. The response cannot simply involve telling the boys that the current situation is unacceptable and must stop. Phillip has too much to lose and Derek might react by rejecting the friendship. Adults must validate the friendship, particularly for Phillip, who values Derek a great deal. Unlike some children who would not accept Derek's behaviour (discussed in more detail on page 69), Phillip does not want to end the friendship and appears to have accepted the bullying behaviour as the price of having this friend. Phillip needs help on both emotional and practical levels.

Emotionally, Phillip needs help to feel more confident, and to feel that he deserves to be treated well. Only then might he be in a position to confront Derek or to make decisions about the friendship. It can be challenging for parents and teachers to refrain from telling Phillip that Derek is "not a friend" and advising him to end the friendship. Adults must understand that it can be extremely difficult for any young person to extract him or herself from a bullying situation, which is far more complicated when those involved are friends. At the same time, an adult response is important. Here, Debra Pepler's concept of scaffolding can be applied to help Phillip boost his feelings of self-worth. Using scaffolding, adults should begin where Phillip feels comfortable, and take small steps to help him feel better about himself. Phillip appears to need adult help in order to deal with and extract himself from this problematic friendship dynamic.

Phillip's intense need for the friendship must be understood, and at the same time he needs to be protected so that he will not continue to tolerate such behaviour. Phillip's apparent tolerance of Derek's treatment suggests that he may need help from a social worker or psychologist. The professional help he receives can be reinforced by parents and teachers, again utilizing scaffolding to help him feel better about himself and make more adaptive choices. Recognizing that addressing Phillip's self-esteem and responses will likely take time, adults need to give him practical help at the same time. For example, they may encourage him to join other groups of peers or clubs. Tying in Pepler's concept of social architecture, adults in Phillip's life may need to structure his social groups in order to promote positive experiences. Phillip could benefit from becoming involved in activities and groups outside of hockey so that he will not be as dependent on Derek. This might broaden his world more immediately and provide him with opportunities to build his self-esteem. It will be critical that these adult responses are subtle and do not further humiliate Phillip; that would only aggravate the situation.

At this point, we do not have enough information to know how to respond to Derek. It is critical, however, that his problematic behaviour be addressed by adults. The challenge is to maintain a fine balance. With Derek, this would mean giving him the message that the bullying behaviour is not acceptable while acknowledging the positive ways he treats Phillip. If possible, an adult can help identify Derek's dilemma—trying to balance his friendship with Phillip and his need for social status among the cool group—in other words, compartmentalizing the two parts of his life.

Case Example 2

Ethan, a grade seven boy who is small for his age and has few friends, recently stumbled upon a website created by three of his peers. The site targeted Ethan and several other boys in his grade also considered unpopular, and appeared to have been created for the sole purpose of making fun of the boys. Soon, Ethan's entire class knew of the website and whispered loudly about him in his presence, laughing at the insults posted online. Ethan felt humiliated and increasingly isolated. Classmates, even some who had previously been quite friendly with the victimized boys, began limiting their interactions with them. No one told the teacher or any parents about the website, and Ethan did not speak to the other victims about it.

A lack of strong friendships may leave young people at risk of victimization and without a protective buffer if they are victimized. Moreover, children tend to want friends who are popular; they will often avoid children who are bullied. Although most children claim to be opposed to bullying, few actually stand up for victimized peers. The discrepancy between what children *say* about bullying and what they *do* about it can be attributed to factors such as self-preservation concerns, fear of retaliation, and the interpersonal challenges of standing up and intervening. In the example above, the other grade seven students may have feared that speaking out would result in their own victimization. Perhaps the perpetrators were part of the "popular crowd" and the other children wanted to be liked and accepted by them. Some students may have felt the website was wrong, and may have felt badly for the victimized boys. As nobody spoke up, however, the victimized boys likely thought they had no support among the rest of the students. With little peer support for the victims, a situation such as this may escalate.[5]

Case Example 3

Becky is a well-liked girl in grade five who has been increasingly distressed by the bullying behaviour of Alice, a girl in her class who she considers a friend. Alice frequently takes her lunch snacks and orders her around in the playground. Despite her apprehension regarding Alice, Becky feels unable to withdraw from the friendship. She is so upset, however, that she told her parents: "Alice always bugs me to just play with her only and she insults my other friends. This makes me angry. But when I don't play with her she makes this super sad face, and I feel bad and can't turn her down." She was afraid to tell the teacher for fear that Alice would find out. Her parents encouraged her to be understanding and empathic toward Alice, as they knew that she was troubled; they were aware of conflict in her home life. They also expressed pride that Becky showed understanding and compassion toward Alice's difficulties.

In this case, Alice was striving to be closer to Becky through control and manipulation. It is common for conflict to occur in friendships among girls, as, by and large, those relationships are more important to them than they are to boys (Catanzaro 2011; Crick & Grotpeter 1995; Crick & Grotpeter 1996). In this example, conflict crossed a line and turned into bullying. It can often be challenging to distinguish "normal conflict" from "bullying," but Becky expressed feeling bullied, and Alice's behaviour was clearly hurtful and repetitive. It went beyond the typical feelings of jealousy that may arise when a friend spends time with another playmate. Becky's parents did not recognize the gravity of the situation. Rather, in their desire to be supportive, they praised Becky and encouraged her to continue the friendship. Feeling guilty and encouraged by her parents to be kind, Becky complied.

Both Alice and Becky seem to need assistance from adults in navigating their relationship. Becky's parents are supportive of their daughter and praise her for her insight and empathy. They may need help, however, to think carefully about how they encourage Becky's positive qualities; they may be inadvertently burdening their daughter. Congratulating her on her empathy and other strengths may have contributed to Becky's sense that she must tolerate Alice's behaviour. Becky's parents may need assistance to manage being supportive of their daughter without unintentionally pressuring her to tolerate Alice's treatment. Scaffolding may be needed for Becky's parents to help them strike this fine balance. In this, it would be important to acknowledge their positive support of Becky.

Alice may need help with her own difficulties; these seem to go beyond her problematic interactions with Becky. She would likely benefit from professional help, which may involve individual or family counselling. Teachers or other adults in her life may identify this need and refer Alice to a social worker or psychologist. An important part of the help would need to include setting limits on her treatment of Becky, in a way that was firm yet empathic.

Case Example 4

Twelve-year-old Fatima has become increasingly upset over the past several months. She had been friends with Rena, a companion since kindergarten, but recently Rena "dropped" Fatima for other friends. Rena began to exclude Fatima in a way that was hurtful. One day, Fatima overheard Rena telling her new friends, "She is so weird, and her family is too. Her brother is a spaz and her parents yell at each other all the time." When they were best friends, Fatima had shared in confidence her distress over her brother's hyper behaviour and her parents' marital conflict. She was devastated to hear Rena break these confidences.

Changes in friendships are common in childhood. Changes can occur as a result of circumstance, such as a change of classroom, school, or neighbourhood. Children may drift apart naturally, with no hard feelings. In some cases, however, children's relationships dissolve or end abruptly on bad terms, which may be associated with bullying. Fatima was not only faced with the loss of a long-time best friend, but experienced bullying by this friend. Fatima required support. Her parents likely noticed her abrupt change in friends and may have inquired about this. Fatima may have disclosed what happened, or alternatively—like many children—may have refrained from disclosing it to adults around her. It is therefore important for parents to be attentive to their children's relationships and attuned to any changes and corresponding shifts in their children's moods or behaviour. For instance, Fatima's parents may have noticed that their daughter had not been to the mall with Rena in some time, previously a weekly ritual. Corresponding to this, they may have noticed that Fatima appeared upset and sad, and was less eager to attend school. Through these cues, it may have become clear to both Fatima's and Rena's parents that there had been a disruption in the friendship.

It is important for the parents of both girls to maintain open lines of communication with their daughters, discuss the apparent friendship breakdown, and provide assistance as needed. Some parents may be cautious about discussing friendship changes with their children, perhaps not wanting to "interfere," or believing it is best to allow children to "work it out." It is critical for parents to communicate with their children in order to understand their social lives. And it may be necessary at times to intervene, while remaining sensitive to the situation and their child's vulnerability. In this situation, Fatima's parents may help her cope with her hurt feelings, and could perhaps speak to Rena about the situation in hopes of bringing an end to the bullying. Fatima likely needs assistance from her parents and perhaps other adults to cope with her confusing feelings about Rena—feelings of hurt, yet at the same time wanting to maintain the friendship. She may benefit from meeting with a professional.

Children at Fatima's age typically begin sharing secrets and private information with friends, relying on them for companionship and support. This is a normal part of development and can contribute to lasting friendship bonds and to building a sense of trust in others. Also at this age, children's social and cognitive skills are rapidly advancing. For some, relationship skills keep pace with these developments and children are able to maintain healthy friendships. For others, healthy relationship skills lag while social and cognitive skills advance.

Rena may have wanted to elevate her social status. She identified that one method was to abandon a long-time friend in order to gain acceptance within a new group of friends. While this behaviour might demonstrate that Rena's social and cognitive skills were developing in some ways, it also reveals a lack of empathy. It seems that she betrayed private information as a tool of manipulation. Without more information, it is not possible to determine the source of Rena's relationship difficulties. Any number of factors may underlie her actions. In order to determine the best mode of intervention, it would be important to further understand what contributed to Rena's behaviour. Rena's parents may start by asking about her recent change in friends, and particularly about the ending of her friendship with Fatima. This may open lines of communication and assist in identifying problems (Stauffacher & DeHart 2006).

Case Example 5

Kim and Jessica, a pair of self-described best friends in grade three, constantly bicker and are often "mean" to one another. Kim is usually more aggressive, spreading rumours about Jessica and threatening to end the friendship at apparently random times. Both the girls' parents and the teacher are aware of the girls' aggressive pattern. At times, the adults separate the two girls.

Such situations may feel exasperating for teachers and parents. Some teachers characterize this as a "fleeting friendship," a relationship that shifts with little warning between hot and cold, between aggression and intimacy. This is a friendship that involves problematic patterns that require intervention. Our study[6] examined bullying from the perspectives of students in grades four and five who identified as victimized, as well as their parents and educators. Children and adults alike commented on the high levels of "conflict" among groups of friends and acquaintances, particularly the girls. One teacher described a situation she observed in this way: "one minute they are best friends and the next minute they're excluding each other and talking behind each other's back." It can be difficult for adults and children to sort out the difference between the "normal" conflict among friends that would characterize many friendships, and situations that constitute bullying. This distinction does matter. Normal conflict can be helpful in building conflict-resolution skills, particularly if this can take place in the context of guidance or advice from adults. Some situations involve bullying, however, and in these instances children should not be left to resolve the conflict on their own. Working through bullying dynamics is often an impossible task for children. This can be the case in particular for those children who are more prone to victimization.

Teachers and parents often assume that conflict in friendships is mutual and that each child is on equal footing. But this may be incorrect. There are often subtle but important differences in power among individual children within a friendship, although these might be hard to detect. The more outspoken or confident child may become a natural leader in a group, and he or she may in turn have more power than the others as a result of social status. More subtle power imbalances also exist among friends. One child may have more power than her friend, for example, because she knows that friend's secrets, yet has shared none of her own. While the former imbalance may be easy for an adult to detect, the latter may be more difficult; here, the girl may or may not be purposefully manipulating this situation to gain power. Her friend may not recognize the imbalance or may be too vulnerable to challenge her friend.

Bullying Among Friends: Additional Findings

In our research, a number of children struggled to determine whether their friend's behaviours constituted bullying or were intended "for fun." One girl described bullying-type behaviour by another girl who she considered to be a friend. After describing the behaviour, she immediately added that it was "just one of those joking things." She also disclosed that she often relinquished her snack to this girl, who would otherwise threaten to end the friendship. Although she complied with her friend's demands, she described feeling "a bit upset every time" and added that she thought the "bully friend" didn't "really mean it." Her experience highlights the complicated and confusing feelings that can result from being victimized by a friend.

Another research participant in grade six described two friends who repeatedly took her lunch and school materials. Despite her distress, the girl tolerated the behaviour, hoping it would stop. She had never before told anyone, and neither the girl's mother nor teacher was aware of the situation. In fact, the girl's teacher was surprised to find this out because she saw the girl as a "confident" and "very content child." The girl seemed to work at believing her friends were "doing it for fun," which she confirmed by rationalizing that they sometimes "talked nicely" with her.

Another girl claimed that her friends did not bully her, yet described a scenario in which at times some of them excluded her, refusing to let her play with them. This both surprised and upset her. This girl's parents and teacher had no idea this was happening. Her teacher described this girl as "well-adjusted and a good student." Many participants in our study told us that they did not tell an adult about being bullied because the perpetrators were also their friends. The victimized children did not want to get them into trouble or, perhaps more importantly, risk losing the friendship.

Our study found that, of those children who were victimized, most had also experienced bullying at the hands of friends. Key differences emerged in their responses and the way bullying affected the friendship. Some of the children considered the bullying behaviour by their friends to be unacceptable. These children reported that they either wanted to stop or had already stopped being friends with that child. The parents and teachers of these children typically described them as well-adjusted, academically excellent, popular, and confident. Analysis of their interviews revealed that they were able to recognize that their friend's behaviour constituted bullying, to consider this behaviour intolerable, and to subsequently end the friendship. Still, despite such clarity and ability to take self-defensive action (and also in spite of the time span between the bullying episodes and the interview), the distress these children had experienced was palpable. One boy who calmly spoke about bullying started to cry as soon as he described the bullying he experienced from his close friend, adding that he felt unable to discuss it further. He had ended the friendship because of the bullying. It is worth noting that he did not have trouble speaking calmly about other issues.

Not all of the children in the study had been able to so easily end their friendships with bullies. Some children who reported bullying by a friend said they wanted to end the friendship but did not know how and could not follow through with their intent. Often, they expressed fear of the consequences of ending the friendship, and hoped that the bullying would subside with time. Some children in the study did not indicate any desire to end the friendship with the children who bullied them. Rather—like Phillip in the example above—not only were they concerned about how the aggressive child felt about them, but they strongly desired continuation of the friendship.

Each child is different, and each situation of bullying among friends is unique. Children respond to these situations in a range of ways due to differences in personality and temperament, as well as differences in context (e.g., home life, previous history of bullying involvement). For instance, a child who has witnessed a great deal of conflict at home and has experienced bullying by peers in the past might be unable to recognize that he or she is being bullied, or that bullying by his or her friends is unacceptable. Alternatively, this child might feel devastated when bullied by a friend. The friendship might have been the only "safe haven" and buffer for this child from a troubled home life and from negative treatment by other peers.

The above examples reveal the extent to which bullying among friends can be detrimental. It may even be more destructive than bullying among peers who are not considered friends. Feelings of betrayal, disappointment, and loneliness might be mixed with anger and sadness. Some victimized children and teenagers might feel they are not worthy of better treatment. It might be confusing, as children wonder whether the friends were just "having fun" or joking around, or if they themselves are somehow responsible. The children may cling to the belief that their friend was joking as a way of avoiding the painful feelings and choices that arise should they recognize the behaviour as bullying. Children may feel particularly isolated, torn between telling an adult and "betraying" a friend. Those who victimize their friends may also face negative consequences. As these children grow older, they might become aggressive with friends, romantic partners, and co-workers.

Siblings and Bullying

Case Example 6

Brothers Frank, age 17, and Cameron, age 13, live with their mother in a small apartment and share a bedroom. For as long as their mother can recall, Frank has been aggressive toward his younger brother. A widowed single parent with few supports, their mother has always been very committed to giving her boys opportunities that she did not have, and works long hours to provide for them. In previous years, their mother protected Cameron when Frank was aggressive toward him. That was before the boys' father passed away unexpectedly, leaving their mother alone, distressed, and the sole provider. She eventually became exhausted from constantly intervening to stop Frank from "picking on" his brother. By the time Cameron entered his teenage years, his mother had stopped protecting him from Frank altogether. She was exasperated and out of ideas about how to prevent Frank's behaviour. Furthermore, her family and friends often criticized her for being overly protective, and she started to doubt herself and fear that this was true. Although she felt guilty and worried about leaving Cameron to protect himself, she rationalized her new hands-off approach by telling herself that Cameron needed to learn how to work it out on his own. Cameron became increasingly scared of his brother, and began to have trouble sleeping and concentrating.

Positive sibling relationships can blur the lines between friends and family and offer lifelong love and support. Early family relationships prepare children to form other kinds of relationships with non-family members later in life. Unlike with friends, children cannot choose their families, and siblings tend to spend a great deal of time together. In this context, children invariably become aware of their siblings' vulnerabilities, knowledge they can sometimes use to tease, control, or gain power over them. In this case, Frank was bullying his younger brother Cameron. There is relatively little research on bullying among siblings, although there is growing interest in this topic. While the family setting is distinct from the peer context, there are commonalities across bullying situations among siblings, friends, and peers. Children involved in bullying with siblings tend to be involved in similar dynamics with others. To understand and determine how to help, it would be important to investigate whether Cameron and Frank are involved in bullying situations with peers or others, and in what roles.

Often dismissed as "normal" or part of growing up, many children and youth are involved in bullying with their siblings. One study found that 78 percent of young adults had been victims of sibling bullying and 85 percent had been perpetrators. Most of these research participants accepted the bullying as normal and did not feel it affected the closeness of their sibling relationships. Many incidents reportedly occurred when their parents were present. Even though sibling bullying was largely regarded as normal, victims often expressed anger, distress, embarrassment, sadness, and even shame about these incidents. Of note, the effect on the victims was often greater than the perpetrators realized. Perhaps Frank minimized or did not recognize the impact of his behaviours. Perhaps he even considered this normal sibling behaviour. Cameron was affected by the victimization, as evidenced by his distress and difficulty sleeping. Further, it was impossible for Cameron to avoid Frank, which contributed to the bullying becoming a source of constant fear and anxiety. Research indeed suggests that sibling bullying can have a negative impact on mental health and can be just as detrimental to victims as peer aggression.[7]

Many of the lessons children learn about relationships come from their families. Parents have a special role in leading by example and demonstrating to children how to relate to others. Those who are warm, positive, and engaged in the lives of their children likely promote healthier relational patterns among siblings. In the case study, the boys' mother was in a difficult situation. Parenting on her own with little support, and with criticism from family and friends, she knew the sibling dynamic was unhealthy and damaging but despite years of trying she had been unable to fix it. The family would benefit from counselling and other supports, but these were difficult for her to access.

Gender and birth order might impact bullying dynamics, as might the individual characteristics of the children in the family such as personality and temperament. Frank naturally held more power because he was older, which afforded him an advantage in both physical size and cognitive maturity. Moreover, his mother often asked him to help out at home, including "babysitting" Cameron with some regularity. The boys' mother felt conflicted and uneasy about this, but had little choice. She desperately needed help with household tasks and could not afford to hire an outside babysitter. As an older brother who was often responsible for Cameron, Frank clearly held a great deal of power.[8]

While families play an important role in teaching children about relationships, young people do not grow up in a vacuum. Parents cannot be assumed to be responsible for their children's involvement in bullying, and other areas of a child's life outside of the family must be examined to identify potential sources for relationship problems. Cameron and Frank may have learned about relationships from countless sources in addition to their family, such as from interacting with others at daycare, school, or in the neighbourhood, or from playing sports, attending summer camp, and regular as well as social media. These boys may have been exposed to both subtle and more obvious lessons about relationships in daily life, in everything from witnessing interactions at the grocery store to watching television. Teachers and other adults are role models; it is important to consider the explicit and implicit messages that these adults may have given Cameron and Frank about relationships.

Strategies for Responding to Bullying Among Siblings

Aggression and conflict in sibling relationships can be easily explained away as part of the normal trials and tribulations of growing up. There are few who cannot recall some degree of fighting or arguing with a brother or sister. We cannot ignore aggression and conflict in sibling relationships, however, particularly when the dynamics among children appear to have qualities of bullying. There are often power differences among siblings, based on factors such as age and size, although this differential may not always appear clear. At times, there is a perceived or actual favoured child in a family, which may also influence power dynamics among siblings.

When bullying situations arise among friends or peers, it is important to question whether bullying is also taking place within the family. Bullying behaviours may begin in the school context and continue at home, or such behaviours may start at home among siblings and continue at school or elsewhere. Perhaps a child is bullied at school and takes out his or her frustration on a sibling when he or she returns home. Alternatively, it may be that a particular class or school condones aggressive behaviour, and in turn, children come to think that bullying is an acceptable way to relate to others; this attitude may then be brought into the home. Problematic patterns may also begin in other contexts, such as extracurricular activities. A particularly competitive and aggressive hockey coach might set a bad example for those on the team, and the behaviour learned at practice might be considered acceptable to a youth, who then may display such behaviour at home and school. These examples may also come from media; for instance, a group of girls may idolize characters from a television show who engage in relational bullying. This may influence how the girls relate to one another and their siblings. Assessing and addressing problems at home, school, and other contexts are crucial to creating long-lasting changes in patterns of relating.[9]

While it is essential to keep in mind that bullying among siblings may stem from issues outside of the home, certain characteristics are amenable to change and likely influence sibling bullying. For instance, addressing general family conflict and hostility might be key to stopping bullying both at home and in other settings. It is also important for parents to recognize when their children are relating in aggressive or problematic ways—regardless of the source—and intervene appropriately. By ignoring or normalizing negative interactions among siblings, parents send the message that it is okay to relate to others in that fashion. Silence on the part of parents might create even more hostility among siblings; one might feel that the other is always "getting away" with bad behaviour, or is favoured in some way.

When a child tells a parent or other adult about being bullied by a sibling, the adult's response is crucial. Invalidating responses may inflict additional damage and deter the child from telling or seeking support in the future. For example, telling a child to stop "tattling" on his or her brother or sister may be a missed opportunity to teach the child that while "tattling" to get a sibling in trouble is unacceptable behaviour, telling an adult about bullying in order to help stop it is encouraged. In Cameron's case, his mother's changed response left him feeling fearful and alone.

Myths and facts

As with bullying among friends, there are several myths about sibling bullying. First, contrary to popular belief, aggression, conflict, and bullying are not "normal" when it comes to siblings. While some level of conflict and irritation is common, repetitive and unbalanced aggression should not be seen as such. It can inflict serious harm on the victimized child and can reinforce negative ways of interacting for the aggressor. It is also commonly believed that bullying is caused by some fault or dysfunction originating in the family. Rather, there are many paths that can lead to bullying among siblings, peers, friends, and acquaintances. Even children who grow up with the best examples of healthy relationships in the family context can become involved in bullying for a variety of reasons. Bullying among siblings can occur even in high-functioning, happy, and healthy families. Finally, it can be harmful to believe that children must learn to resolve sibling conflict independently. Adults cannot expect young people to have the ability and perspective to resolve bullying issues on their own. Adult intervention may be required and can be beneficial. At the very least, adults must be mindful of the interactions and make conscious choices about how to respond. Adults can play an important role in offering support to the distressed child, repairing the damage the bullying has caused, and implementing meaningful consequences at home and perhaps in other settings in order to stop the bullying behaviour and teach more adaptive ways of acting.

Concluding Comments

Experiencing bullying at the hands of a friend can be distressing and confusing for the victimized child. It can be difficult for children and adults to identify bullying within friendships. Even when children recognize that they are being bullied by a friend, they may rationalize or minimize the behaviour. If they recognize the behaviour as bullying, they might not know how to respond, or alternatively they might accept the behaviour in order to maintain the friendship. Bullying among siblings can be just as hurtful and harmful as bullying among peers, and it can be difficult for children to escape sibling bullying because of the amount of time that family members spend with one another.

Children and adults may be less likely and more reluctant to judge behaviour as bullying when the behaviour occurs among friends or siblings. Adults might believe that leaving children to their own devices in navigating these relationships is a good way to foster growth. However, adults have an important role to play in helping children and youth deal with the dilemmas associated with bullying among friends and siblings, and in helping them develop and sustain healthy relationships. Attention to children's patterns of relating is key to identifying bullying within friendships and sibling relationships. Modelling healthy relationship skills is also important. The key concepts of scaffolding and social architecture can help adults respond to bullying in an ongoing fashion, be it bullying among friends and siblings or bullying in general. Once problematic patterns are identified, adults must respond sensitively, balancing children's wishes with taking action to resolve harmful situations.

Chapter 5

Bullying: Who Knew It Was So Complex!

Introduction

We have seen in previous chapters how bullying can take many forms: it can be direct or indirect, verbal, physical, relational, or cyber. In some cases, it is motivated by bias or hatred toward particular individuals or groups. It can occur among friends, peers, siblings—the victim may never even know the bully's identity. Regardless of form, bullying is complex. It is no wonder that finding solutions is rarely easy. Recognizing and understanding the many complexities, however, is an important starting point in working toward a solution. This chapter draws on several examples that highlight these complexities and considers possible approaches. We then introduce the ecological framework, a comprehensive theoretical approach that can help us understand and respond effectively in bullying situations.

Case Example 1
Courtney: "It's Just a Game!"

Courtney is a well-liked and kind-hearted eight-year-old girl. She recently came home from school and asked her mother, Julie, if they could bake cookies for a class celebration the next day. When asked about the celebration, Courtney said it was "Queen Suzie Day," part of a "game" some students in the class played. Courtney explained that her classmate Suzie was the queen and that a few of the students had to do everything she said. If someone refused a request by the queen, Suzie sent a note to the others in the group saying that they could not talk to the "traitor." If someone disobeyed the queen they might be beat up after

continued

school by Josh, the king. With questioning, Julie found out that the teacher did not know about this "game" and that Josh had pushed around a couple of boys who had refused Suzie's requests. Julie was further dismayed to hear that her daughter had been giving Suzie her lunch snacks for the past month—also unbeknownst to the teacher—and that she always complied with Suzie's requests. Although Courtney did not seem at all distressed while speaking about this so-called game, Julie felt troubled and told her daughter that this game sounded like bullying. This upset Courtney; she insisted that she enjoyed the game. She became more upset when Julie told her she was going to tell the teacher.

In this case, Julie had to grapple with some difficult questions and decisions. She had to decide what to say to her daughter, and whether (and how) to approach the teacher and other parents. It was clear to her that the game was highly problematic. Puzzled by her daughter's apparent lack of concern, Julie wondered if, because of her age, Courtney lacked the maturity to recognize that she was being bullied. Julie had the challenging task of explaining to her daughter how she saw the situation without causing further upset, particularly since for the most part Courtney appeared to be a confident and happy child who interacted well with her peers.

Julie had many questions, most of which she was unable to answer. She wondered how the other children felt about the game. She thought it likely that few if any really did enjoy playing it, particularly those who refused Suzie's requests and in turn were excluded, threatened, and at times hurt. She wondered what was making Suzie and Josh act this way and believed that if their behaviour was unaddressed or regarded as normal "child's play," these patterns could worsen and escalate when they became teenagers and adults. She wanted to know whether the other children's parents knew about the game and, if so, how they reacted upon learning about Queen Suzie. Julie knew that adult responses influence how children understand interpersonal relationships.

Concerned that after more than a month the teacher did not know about these interactions among the children, Julie wondered if the school tolerated such behaviour. On the other hand, herself a busy professional, Julie knew that the demands of teaching made it hard to attend to everyday student interactions. It crossed her mind that the teacher might be aware of the game but not concerned about it. Julie realized that if she approached the school, she needed to do so as an ally trying to work together to address the situation, doing so without putting Courtney on the spot.

This case illustrates several of the complexities inherent in bullying situations. In this scenario, as in other cases of bullying, it may be challenging to detect and fully understand the power relations among children in the classroom or other contexts. Clearly, Suzie holds a great deal of social power. What is it about Suzie that allows her to yield such power? It may be her self-confidence or social skills, or other difficult-to-define relationship and leadership qualities. Ironically, these are all positive qualities that parents typically hope to see in their children. But Suzie is using these potentially valuable qualities in ways that contribute to unhealthy relational patterns.

When responding, it is important that adults do so in a way that does not discourage or dampen Suzie's positive qualities. It is also critical that strategies and responses take into account the child's developmental stage. For instance, using the scaffolding technique (Pepler 2006) introduced in Chapter 4, Suzie's teacher and parents might assess her strengths in addition to her problematic behaviour with peers. Suzie may benefit from an approach that primarily focuses on redirecting her leadership abilities into positive, pro-social behaviour. She also needs help to realize why the game is problematic and must not continue. The challenge is to help Suzie shift her behaviour without causing her to feel humiliated. Feeling humiliated can foster negative feelings, which could further entrench her bullying behaviours. Rather, Suzie's parents and teachers could focus on supporting and encouraging her positive leadership and healthy relationship skills. For example, she could be designated the class helper during activities such as arts and crafts, and her role could be to hand out materials, check if any classmates require more tools or supplies, and ensure everything is returned at the end. If this is insufficient, Suzie may require some counselling with a social worker or psychologist. It might be advisable for Suzie's parents and teacher to remain vigilant, but in a supportive way, in order to support and encourage her healthy relationship skills.

It is just as important to understand the strengths as well as the needs of the victims in bullying situations. Courtney clearly has many strengths: she possesses a generous, easy-going temperament, in addition to an uncommon ability to see the best in others. When discussing the situation with Courtney, it would be important not to dampen any of these positive qualities. Rather, they should be fostered, alongside lessons focused on the idea of respect and mutuality in relationships, and delivered in a way that is tailored to her developmental stage. Her parents may find opportune times to emphasize that Courtney has the right to be treated with respect. For instance, if Courtney's parents learn that she gave her snack to another child, they may inquire about whether the two children "swapped" snacks. They can encourage and support her sharing behaviour, while also noting the benefits of "swapping"; in this scenario each child will get a snack, rather than one child enjoying two snacks while Courtney is left with none. In addition, her parents may take the opportunity to highlight positive and negative relationships when watching television shows or movies with

Courtney. It might also prove helpful for her teacher to structure classroom activities that encourage mutual respect and care, which would benefit both Courtney and Suzie. For instance, a classroom activity might involve students pairing up, each completing a defined task, and then coming together to share what they accomplished and learn from one another. Her teacher may also attempt to encourage assertiveness in Courtney and others. As with Suzie, if these strategies are not sufficient, Courtney may require more intervention, such as referral to a counsellor for assertiveness training.

With this and other situations, it is best if adults focus on empowering all children involved and continuously building and reinforcing positive relationship skills. Adults must avoid humiliating or embarrassing the children, both victims and perpetrators. Attending to interactions among children and recognizing their diverse strengths and needs are key tasks in promoting healthy relationships.

Case Example 2
Edward: "The New Kid"

Edward is a 15-year-old boy who recently immigrated to Canada from Hong Kong with his family. He is friendly with his peers but has not yet made close friends at school. The school cafeteria offers typical Canadian fare, such as grilled cheese sandwiches and burgers, which most students purchase for lunch. Edward's mother packs his lunches at home; they consist of leftovers from traditional Hong Kong dinners. In his largely racially homogenous school, Edward stands out. A couple of peers in the cafeteria often exclaim, loudly enough for others to hear, "Ew! Why does that food smell so bad?" or whisper just loud enough for Edward to hear, "You know, in China they eat dog, I bet that's what he's eating." The lunch monitor does not appear to pay attention and no students stand up for Edward. He begins to feel miserable, hate school, and resent his parents for bringing him to Canada.

What should Edward do in this situation? His first impression of life in Canada is not promising. He is experiencing bullying based on his cultural background; this, as we have seen, is a violation of his rights. Although some of the students who witness the bullying might feel bad for Edward, unless they say something he will likely think all students are against him. The lunch monitor appears to be oblivious to his distress, so it seems that the best intervention will be for Edward to tell an adult. The most likely scenario is that Edward will ignore his tormenters for as long as he can stand it, and only tell his parents or a teacher if it "really" starts to bother him or interfere with his daily activities. In the meantime, his parents might begin to notice that Edward is more irritable and less motivated to attend school. They might think it's natural with such a big move or they might feel confused and concerned about the change in his behaviour. They may be unsure how to help him, since they are also new and adjusting to life in Canada. For instance, they might not feel confident enough in their language abilities to be able to approach the school. If Edward does not recount his experiences at school, it will be difficult for adults to assist in bringing an end to the bullying.

Apparently minor changes at the school could be quite helpful. The lunch monitor could play a more active role, perhaps by observing student interactions more closely, walking around the cafeteria to monitor behaviour, and generally finding ways to be approachable. The school could benefit from cultural awareness workshops or class curriculum that teaches about and celebrates diversity. Further, this school would likely benefit from bullying workshops, particularly those that inform students in an age-appropriate way about their human rights, in addition to strategies that help young people intervene when they witness something troubling.

Workshops are helpful but are not enough to cause change. The school climate likely needs to change as well, given that these seemingly isolated lunchtime interactions will be less likely to occur if this type of behaviour is not supported by a larger environment. The climate in any given school is created by a wide array of factors. Identifying factors that contribute to a hostile, xenophobic, and closed-minded school climate is the first step in preventing and ending the type of bullying that Edward has experienced. Although it takes time and resources, a key goal is to create a school climate that promotes inclusion, celebrates diversity, and cultivates genuine interest and excitement among young people to explore the world and meet its inhabitants, all of whom are equal.

A helpful beginning may be to assess the school climate and prioritize areas of need. The Promoting Relationships and Eliminating Violence Network (PREVNet), Canada's authority on research and resources for bullying prevention, offers a helpful assessment tool for schools. This tool, called PREVNet's BEST, focuses on promoting a healthy and positive school climate and meets mandatory legislative regulatory requirements for assessing school climate. This simple-to-use tool can provide schools with insight on the effectiveness of current anti-bullying efforts and offer strategies to decrease bullying (PREVNet 2014). Changing the entire school climate is invariably a complicated and resource-intensive process. Assessments such as PREVNet's BEST, however, can help school administrators identify priorities and determine where to begin. Beginning small and advancing step by step, school administrators can work toward making larger and more complex changes, ultimately improving the school climate.

Instances of discriminatory or bias-based bullying can be used as teachable moments for young people. It is not enough to hold a workshop or have a policy against bias and discrimination. Rather, children and youth will benefit most from moment-to-moment teaching, in which adults take notice and utilize incidents as opportunities to address problematic language and behaviour as they happen, in ways that do not humiliate the children or youth. Edward's situation would likely improve if adults at the school and in the community took greater advantage of responding to problematic incidents—including even apparently minor ones—and engaged in the challenging task of turning them into teachable moments (Mishna, Newman, Daley, & Solomon 2009).

Case Example 3
Sarah: "A Good Sport"

Sarah, age 11, recently revealed to her two best friends, Kate and Leah, that she had a "serious" crush on a popular boy in their class, Adam. The three girls usually got along well but, at times, Sarah felt excluded. Although she never confronted Kate and Leah, she suspected that they purposely did things to make her feel left out. A few weeks after Sarah told them how she felt about Adam, she walked into class one morning to hear Kate saying loud enough for everyone within earshot to hear, "Sarah loves Adam! Sarah loves Adam!" A number of students erupted in laughter, and Sarah felt humiliated and betrayed. Tears came to her eyes, and she ducked into her seat with her head down and eyes averted. The teacher told everyone to quiet down and moved on to the daily curriculum. Later that day, Sarah checked her Facebook and saw that Leah had written a public status update saying, "Sarah loves Adam! Adam you better run for your life, she is such a loser." She also found a private message from Kate and Leah telling her that they were "just having fun" and knew she would be a "good sport" about it. Sarah felt torn. On the one hand, she felt hurt by her so-called best friends; on the other hand, she felt they usually treated her well, and so was compelled to push her hurt feelings away. She became even more confused when a quiet classmate came over to sit with her at lunch, opening with, "That was so not cool. Kate and Leah can be really mean."

This incident was understandably very upsetting for Sarah. She felt betrayed by her friends and embarrassed that her private feelings were shared publicly, at an age when romantic feelings are just beginning to bloom. She was confused and unsure whether she should be angry. If they were just joking, she worried that her anger would make her appear oversensitive.

Sarah's parents were also unsure about these friendships. Her mother in particular found that although both Kate and Leah were polite, they sometimes said things and acted in ways that she thought were hurtful to her daughter. This reaction irritated Sarah, who assured her mother they were joking. After the classroom incident, Sarah was noticeably withdrawn and distressed; this concerned her parents. Sarah denied that anything was wrong and, although she felt tempted to tell her parents in order to receive desperately needed comfort, she feared they would try to prevent her from being friends with Kate and Leah. Although she had a family that could be a crucial support, it was unlikely that she would tell them about the incident.

Parents and teachers must be viewed as safe havens where children can turn when distressed. There are many complex reasons children do not disclose their experiences of victimization, some of which are related to adults. Sarah's parents are in a difficult position. They are alert to and concerned about this problematic friendship. They will soon need to recognize, however, that because of their daughter's age they do not have the same ability to control her social life as in her earlier years. If they respond by advising her to end her friendships with Kate and Leah, for example, they will only be putting their daughter in a position that could force her to defy them. In addition, she may stop sharing distressing incidents with them, understanding that they want the best for her yet feeling unable to follow their suggestions. Rather, her parents can opt to express concern about these friendships, help her respond to Kate and Leah's behaviours, and continue to carefully monitor their daughter's interactions, all the while maintaining a supportive attitude. At the same time, they may try to understand factors that could be contributing to their daughter's vulnerability to being in this situation; this could help them develop a plan to move forward and assist their daughter in learning healthy relationship skills.

Even though Kate had spoken loudly, there was a buzz in the room before the class began and the teacher was preoccupied with preparing the class material, which may have kept him or her from noticing the behaviour. If the teacher had noticed, she or he may have thought little of the incident because Sarah was popular and a good student—not someone who would typically be considered vulnerable. This type of stereotyping can lead to adults missing important opportunities for intervention. Had the teacher realized how hurt Sarah was regardless of her popular status, he/she could have discreetly asked her to stay after class to check whether there was something wrong. In this conversation with the teacher, Sarah may have insisted everything was okay and that would be the end of it. Alternatively, the teacher may have noticed her demeanour and recommend that she talk to the social worker or guidance counsellor, even if only on a single occasion. This could also be a perfect time to hold a talk or presentation about excluding and hurting others, for the class or even the whole school, without putting any one individual on the spot. The incident might serve as a helpful signal that the children in the class require assistance in developing and maintaining friendships. Attending to the social-emotional needs and strengths of students may go a long way to fostering healthy relationship skills.

Sarah's classmate showed courage and empathy in approaching her the next day. This sent a message to Sarah that everyone was not laughing at her and that perhaps those classmates who kept quiet did not necessarily approve of Kate and Leah's behaviour. This could be the start of a new friendship for Sarah, leaving her less dependent on Leah and Kate. This positive bystander behaviour is a strength that can be fostered further in the classroom and in the school. Bystander behaviour is related to the overall school climate, and therefore assessing the climate and addressing areas of need may be important for Sarah's school.

Case Example 4
Kevin: The Bowling Club

Kevin and Steve are both age six and in the same grade one class. Steve recently invited Kevin to his Bowling Club get-together, but told him not to tell anyone about it because a few boys in the class were not invited. Sheila, Kevin's mother, found this strange but did not think a great deal about it. Kevin attended the club meeting that weekend. A few days later, Steve's mother Joan called Sheila with the "good news": Kevin was permitted to join the Bowling Club. Sheila learned that this club had been going on all year, and had been established by Joan as a way of helping her son make more friends. With the exception of Kevin and two other boys, all the boys in the class had been part of the Bowling Club for the entire year. Joan had asked the boys in the club not to talk about it at school so that the others wouldn't find out. When Sheila asked why the invitation was not extended to all the boys in the class, Joan hesitated and explained that it would be too much to host that many children each month. Sheila was shocked; she responded that she did not want her son being part of an exclusionary club. Joan insisted that it was not exclusionary, and certainly not intended to hurt others. None of the other mothers had found this to be a concern, said Joan coldly; there was an implication that Sheila was being oversensitive because her son had not been initially included.

Sheila was quite angry. She felt that although the Bowling Club was presented as a benign activity, this type of exclusionary practice set the stage for future bullying and relationship problems. She believed that Joan and the other mothers were teaching the boys that it is okay to exclude others. She thought that in a few years some of the boys might act as bullies; perhaps nobody would be able to see the link with their parents' behaviour years earlier with respect to the Bowling Club. Even though she was upset and concerned about the club, Sheila was unsure what to do next. She had made it clear to Joan that she would not tolerate exclusionary behaviour. She wondered if she should take this matter further and considered approaching the teacher. She was very concerned about her son and the other boys in grade one and was convinced that the long-standing existence of this club meant there was a need for a broader intervention on encouraging healthy relationships. She felt strongly that the parents needed a workshop. Sheila contemplated speaking more with Joan to stress how important it was to promote an inclusive peer group.

We do not usually talk about parents' roles in bullying incidents. In this scenario, Sheila was able to recognize that a parent was fostering exclusionary behaviour. Only six years old, the children were too young to understand why such a club could be hurtful to those not included. Joan had been concerned about her son having friends, although she did not demonstrate insight into the potentially negative impact of excluding some children from the club. Sheila might find it helpful to speak with Joan again. Her initial conversation may have caught Joan off-guard, and Joan may have reacted defensively simply because she had never before considered that her behaviour could have a negative impact on the children in her son's class. Although it would be difficult, Sheila might try to approach the conversation in a calmer manner, without casting blame on Joan.

It is possible, however, that another conversation with Joan would be no more productive. Sheila might then decide to approach the school and request some sort of strategy that could address the exclusionary behaviour. She might request that the teacher attend to the behaviours and group activities of the children in the class, paying particular attention to how the Bowling Club members behave to identify points of intervention. She might also request that programming aimed at the parents be implemented. While the school cannot force Joan or any other parent to participate in such programming, it may be helpful in raising awareness of the ways that parents can actually inadvertently promote bullying behaviour. Don't forget, there were many other parents who allowed their children to attend the Bowling Club, seeing no problem with it. Addressing their complicit role in the exclusion is important, in addition to Joan's more active role, in a manner that does not lay blame or cause them embarrassment. If all parents receive a consistent message about the negative impact of exclusionary behaviour, more of them may be able to recognize and even articulate concerns with social clubs like the Bowling Club. They may be more cautious about allowing their children to attend and more confident in challenging such clubs. Seemingly small changes in parental behaviour can contribute to a more positive school and community climate that inhibits rather than fosters exclusionary behaviour.

Several high-profile cases involving the non-consensual distribution of intimate images have appeared in recent years. These cases have received

Case Example 5
Laura: "Revenge Porn"

Laura and her brother Adam attend the same high school, Laura in grade 12 and Adam in grade 9. One day near the end of his first semester, a friend of Adam's commented that he had never thought of his sister in "that way." Adam was irked by his friend's comment, but he learned where it came from when he arrived home—where his parents were distraught and angry and his sister was crying. Adam learned that Laura had sent a "sexy" photo of herself to her boyfriend before they broke up, which the ex-boyfriend had posted to his Instagram feed that morning with the hashtag "#slut." By the end of the day, it had circulated around the school, including to teachers and school administrators, who had called the parents of both Laura and her ex. Laura's parents were extremely disappointed in her, claiming they had expected her to "know better." They had given her cyber-safety tip sheets and always restricted computer use. They told Laura that they had done all they could, but even so, she had ignored their counsel. They also called her a "disgrace" to their family, confiscated her phone and laptop, and changed the passwords on their family desktop computer. Laura became increasingly anxious and worried about how her photo had been circulated in the cyber world, and her lack of access to technology began to intensify these feelings. At school the next day, Laura felt very self-conscious and miserable, worried that others might be talking about her. She used her lunch hour to search the web for her image on the library computer, fearing that it had spread further. When Laura returned home, greatly distressed, her parents became very concerned about her emotional state. At the same time, they remained angry. Laura locked herself in her room and refused to attend school the next day.

widespread media attention. The detrimental effects of the non-consensual distribution of private images are clear, and for this reason parents and policy makers alike are urgently trying to prevent and address this issue. As part of these efforts, in November 2013 the Justice Minister introduced the Protecting Canadians from Online Crime Act ("Bill C-13"). Among other items, this bill will make it a crime to transmit intimate images of a person without his or her knowledge or consent.[1] Of course, this alone cannot solve the problem. Prevention and intervention efforts will be most successful if aimed at multiple targets, such as the school, the community, the family, as well as the youth involved in such situations.

Any parent faced with this situation would feel upset. Laura's parents were distraught and confused. They believed that they had prepared their daughter well, and considered her to be a smart and "reasonable" girl who typically demonstrated good judgment. They could not understand how she had made this choice and thought it was important to punish her; the punishment that they chose was to deny Laura access to technology. Children and youth often fear that they will lose this access; this is one of the factors that can prevent them from telling adults about problematic situations in the cyber world. A more helpful approach might be to more carefully monitor Laura's online and social media behaviour, not simply block her access. Her parents may need help accepting that although strategies and rules are essential, there are inevitable risks associated with the cyber world, and there must be a contingency plan that includes going to her parents and learning how to problem solve.

Laura sending the "sexy" photo was inconsistent with her usual behaviour, so it is important to explore the reasons for this uncharacteristic action. She likely cannot articulate why she sent the picture. Girls engage in this type of behaviour for a variety of reasons. In Laura's case, she may have felt pressured to send her boyfriend the photo. Based on her history, it is likely she resisted his requests at first, feeling it was inappropriate. It could be that over time the boy's repeated requests for a photo and insistence that "girls have done that for his friends" wore her down. She may have worried that if she didn't send her boyfriend a photo he might "drop" her. Like many teenage girls, Laura often felt self-conscious and critical of what she perceived to be her flaws. Her boyfriend might have persuaded her using flattery and other means; this might have resulted in Laura ignoring her own usual good sense.

Laura likely needs help exploring what occurred in the dynamics with this boy that led her to comply with his wishes in spite of her original hesitation to do so. It is also important that she understand that the boy had no right to distribute the photo; in actuality, he broke the law. In addition, she needs help exploring the factors that left her vulnerable to the boy's manipulation.

Due to the gravity of this situation and the pain it caused, Laura may require assistance from a social worker or counsellor in order to explore her motives for sending the photo and to cope with the aftermath. In the wake of this incident, Laura was very distressed and began avoiding school. Although the picture had been removed from Instagram, she feared it had been distributed elsewhere online. She felt a constant desire to search for the image, compelled to find it but at the same time fearing that it would surface. For quite some time, whenever she saw a smart phone or computer she was reminded that her picture was "out there." She needed help coping in order to overcome this traumatic incident.

It is important for both Laura and her parents to recognize the complex factors that led to her agreeing to send the photo. Until this point, Laura had shown good judgment; this incident was a signal to her parents that they needed to re-evaluate their trust in their daughter. Her parents might wonder if they had "done something wrong" to make her so vulnerable. It may be important for her parents to work with a social worker or counsellor. Understanding that such incidents occur more often in the new cyber world will not take away their pain, but it may help them understand the context in which Laura's behaviour took place. Perhaps their disappointment could be mitigated. Knowing her parents' trust in her had wavered, Laura feared they "hated" her and thought she was "disgusting." She was very disappointed in herself. Counselling for Laura and her parents may help them cope with this distressing situation and rebuild trust.

The school had a responsibility to address the situation. Depending on the initial reaction, Laura's parents might need to approach the administrators to discuss an appropriate response to the boy's behaviour. The school may decide to suspend the boy and/or implement other interventions focused on bullying, cyberbullying, and cyber behaviour. Depending on Laura's wishes and the school's response, her parents may decide to approach the police. It would also be important for school administration/teachers to expand the focus from Laura's situation. This would entail examining and addressing the context and role of the broader school culture/environment with regards to issues such as students posting private photos without the consent of the person portrayed, as well as the response of bystanders upon viewing such photos.

Case Example 6
Shayne: "The Bystander"

Carole and Allison, long-time partners, contacted a children's mental health agency to request help with their 14-year-old son Shayne. While they had a happy family overall and enjoyed a strong network of family and friends, their son had become "rude" and "moody" since beginning high school. Carole said that when they had finally become "fed up" and asked what was going on, Shayne said he hated his family and wished they were "normal." Shocked and furious, Carole recounted yelling at him and telling him that his behaviour was "rude, disrespectful, and unacceptable." Allison said the situation with Shayne had deteriorated to the point where most conversations escalated into a "yelling match." The family explained that prior to this there had been little conflict in the family. Shayne continued to do well at school, but became angry when either parent spoke to him.

Over the course of several sessions working alone with Shayne, a social worker learned that homophobic bullying was occurring at his new high school. For instance, female athletes were frequently called "dykes" and boys were often called "sissies" or "fags" as put-downs. According to Shayne, teachers and school staff sometimes intervened, but at other times seemed to "pretend not to hear." Shayne's response when he heard this discriminatory language was to feel angry at his moms and wish they had a "normal" family. After some time discussing the situation with the social worker, Shayne began to feel comfortable talking about this with his parents. Carole and Allison were outraged that the school allowed such abuse. Together with the social worker, they discussed strategies for approaching the school.

In this case, Shayne was witnessing homophobic bullying at his new high school, which was causing him to feel distressed and ashamed of his family. These feelings spurred his rude behaviour toward his parents; this in turn was generating considerable family conflict. Proactive in addressing this conflict, Carole and Allison sought help from a children's mental health agency, which proved to be helpful in identifying the issues at work. The social worker noted that bias-based bullying was occurring at the school level, which was negatively affecting Shayne as a bystander. Even though the bullying was not directed toward him specifically, the hurtful language had a profound impact on his well-being.

Shayne required help coping with his feelings of distress, shame, and embarrassment. He desperately wanted to hide the identity of his family from his new peers at school. The social worker helped him to process these feelings and realize that it was his peers and his school that needed to change, rather than his family. Although Shayne eventually agreed to allow his parents to approach the school, he was adamant that he did not want to be identified as a "tattle" or a "narc." His parents decided to contact his homeroom teacher to discuss the situation and determine a strategy for addressing the problematic and biased behaviour occurring in the school. Carole and Allison, together with the social worker, decided to focus on several points. The first goal was to inform the teacher about their family background to make it clear why homophobic comments were hurtful to Shayne, even if not directed at him specifically. Second, Carole and Allison wanted to learn what, if any, policies or rules were in place in the school regarding biased language and bullying in general. They felt this might be a helpful starting point to identify areas in which change could occur to improve the school climate. Depending on how the conversation went with the teacher, Shayne's parents planned to approach the administration to further discuss strategies for improving the school climate, encouraging teachers and school staff to carefully attend to the language used by students, and fostering an environment in which both adults and students alike stand up to biased and discriminatory language and behaviour.

An Expanded Ecological Systems Framework

The young people described in the examples above, just like all children and teenagers, have grown up in their own families, peer groups, schools, communities, and cultures. Each young person is situated within a unique context, which influences their psychosocial development and their relationships. The ecological systems theoretical framework, originally developed by Urie Bronfenbrenner, provides a helpful roadmap to understanding how layered and interacting social contexts influence developing young people.

According to Bronfenbrenner (1979, 1994), human development occurs through a process of progressively complex reciprocal interactions between an active and evolving person and the individuals, objects, and symbols in her or his immediate environment. He argues that it is the enduring interactions occurring over extended periods of time, such as parent-child interactions and play with peers and friends, that affect developing individuals. Depending on a variety of factors within a person and their environment, developmental outcomes will differ.

The ecological environment is thought of as a set of nested structures, with the innermost level termed the *microsystem*. A *microsystem*, in the most basic sense, is the immediate environment in which a person develops, which may include the family, school, and peer group. It includes interpersonal relationships as well as characteristics of the immediate environment that promote or inhibit progressively more complex interaction with this environment. Bronfenbrenner proposed that the various *microsystems* are linked, and further that the immediate environment in which a child develops is linked with various other settings as well. For instance, although children generally do not attend their parents' places of employment, the workplace climates and characteristics most certainly affect the family and child. Surrounding the *microsystem* is the *macrosystem*, according to Bronfenbrenner. As the name implies, the *macrosystem* represents the larger cultures or subcultures that surround a developing child, and may include belief systems, customs, knowledge, lifestyles, opportunity structures, hazards, and life course options. Bronfenbrenner also wanted to capture the temporal dimension of child development, so he identified a *chronosystem* as part of the ecological model. This *chronosystem* represents change or consistency over time in the characteristics of the individual and her or his environment.

In recent years, several scholars[2] have adapted the ecological systems theoretical framework to keep pace with the technological revolution, which has created a new environment in which young people learn and grow: the cyber world.[3] Johnson and Puplampu (2008) propose that theoretical models of child development require attention to the contemporary tools and environments of children. Given that children are now immersed in technology, these scholars identify a *techno-subsystem* as part of the *microsystem* that Bronfenbrenner originally proposed. Martin (2010, 2013) and Martin and colleagues (2011, 2013) suggest that the ecology of the child needs to be expanded to include cyberspace as a system of influence, and they added a distal ring to Bronfenbrenner's ecological systems model to represent the cyber system.

The necessity of these expansions is clear when considering the far-reaching impact of information and communication technology on children and youth.

Recognizing the significance of these developments and adaptations to the ecological framework, we concur that an expanded ecological systems framework is most relevant in assisting us in understanding and responding to bullying among children and adolescents. Further, as Martin and Alaggia (2013) suggest, the framework is consistent with the social work approach of viewing each person in his or her environment. Within this framework, *individual factors* include a child's biological, psychological, and interpersonal strengths and challenges that may result from genetic factors or environmental experiences. These may include characteristics that identify an individual—for example, race, gender, sexual orientation, or disability status. Other individual factors include temperament and stress reactivity, both of which can significantly influence a child's vulnerability to bullying and response to victimization. Social, cognitive, emotional, and relationship skills are other individual factors that are influential in both the risk of involvement in bullying and the reaction to it. Importantly, these individual characteristics are not static and unchanging. When considering intervention approaches, it is important to identify individual characteristics of bullies and victims that create vulnerabilities for these children and heighten their risk for involvement in bullying. It may be helpful to consider which factors are most amenable to change and focus efforts on addressing these.

A crucial part of the environment in which children grow and develop is the family. In the expanded ecological systems framework, *familial influences* include the characteristics of specific family members and their interactions, as well as family structure. Other family factors include family norms and values, attachment relationships, cultural traditions, communication patterns, and conflict resolution strategies. All of these factors may influence a child's involvement in bullying. For instance, a boy may have a very difficult time disclosing his victimization experiences to his family because he is worried they will think he is "weak" or "feminine." These concerns may stem from growing up in a family where pride, strength, and traditional Western concepts of masculinity were emphasized. That is not to say that his family did something wrong or contributed to his victimization, but rather that his family environment may influence how he copes with bullying, which should be a point of consideration. Cultural traditions and backgrounds are other important family factors that can influence bullying involvement. For instance, the term "bullying" is not used or applied across the globe, and there are varying interpretations of this phenomenon and its effects. If a family originates in a culture that does not recognize bullying in the same way it is viewed in Canada, parents and children may react differently to situations of bullying. It is important to stress that one interpretation of bullying is not more correct, but that family culture is an important consideration. Communication patterns and conflict-resolution strategies are other factors that have a fairly obvious link to bullying. Children can learn ways of relating and resolving conflict from many sources, which can interact with the patterns already established in a family and also influence bullying involvement.

Peer influences include peer group relationships and dynamics. It is important to remember that children bring all of their individual characteristics and their family backgrounds to the peer group context, and that factors at each of these three levels can interact and influence one another and bullying involvement. Peer groups tend to develop their own norms and value systems, which can include acceptance or rejection of certain behaviours. Depending on the dynamics, a particular peer group may value strong relationships and reject exclusion or hierarchical membership, or alternatively, a peer group may value popularity above all else. These dynamics and value systems, along with many other factors, can influence whether bullying behaviour emerges and can also influence the way peer group members respond to incidents when they occur. For instance, does the peer group environment support those individual children who decide to stand up for those who are victimized? Or instead, are helpful bystanders outcast and excluded if they try to intervene in bullying situations? Peer group relations are complex to understand and to change, but can be powerful tools in decreasing—or, alas, increasing—bullying behaviours.

Factors such as school climate, leadership, and policies comprise *school influences*. While concepts such as school climate are intangible and difficult to precisely define and understand, school policies are more concrete and easy to interpret. School climate is the result of countless factors that come together and interact, and include the implicit and explicit norms and values expressed at a school, the acceptance of diversity present by teachers and administrators, and the day-to-day interactions among students. For instance, a student who identifies as lesbian may feel that the school climate is accepting and supportive of sexual minorities if derogatory use of the term "gay" is explicitly challenged. She may feel that the school is hostile, however, if gay-straight alliances are banned or restricted at her school, for instance, and derogatory language is frequently used in the hallways with no intervention. One factor that influences school climate is the leadership and administration within a given school. Not surprisingly, school administration can also influence bullying. School administrators in Canada typically recognize how important it is to implement bullying prevention and intervention. But an important question remains: do school administrators take specific incidents of bullying seriously? Likewise, do teachers have ongoing opportunities to participate in continuing education focused on identifying and intervening in bullying situations? The explicit and implicit messages sent by school administrators are important in influencing bullying dynamics as well as prevention and intervention efforts.

The *community and cultural context* includes the availability of resources and supports. This may include the presence of community centres, recreational services, counselling and other supports, and cultural centres. Communities that are rich in services and supports may buffer the impact of bullying for some young people, as well as offer many other benefits to development and well-being. For instance, children may have more opportunities to interact with peers and others if they live in a community with a variety of affordable and accessible recreational activities for growing children and teens. In some communities, participating in activities such as swimming, dance, volleyball, hockey, and drama may be much more accessible than others. These activities may offer young people a variety of opportunities to develop healthy relationship skills. At the same time, we must remember that bullying occurs in these settings as well, and it is important to coordinate efforts among community services, the school, and the family to promote consistent and effective responses. Other services are also important, such as counselling and cultural services. A victimized youth or a perpetrator may require counselling, which may not be accessible if the closest counsellor is located one hour away and outside the reach of public transit. Or, a counsellor may be close in proximity but the fees are not affordable. Cultural services are another important community resource, and they can offer solace for victimized young people and support healthy relationship skills among those who bully others. For instance, a teen who is new to Canada from Mexico may feel isolated and alone, which may increase her vulnerability to victimization. If this teen has access to a Mexican community in which she feels at home and welcomed, this vulnerability may be mitigated. Likewise, a child who displays aggressive and controlling tendencies with his friends may benefit, for example, from becoming a counsellor-in-training at a summer camp, which may emphasize leadership skills and responsibility—areas which include treating others with kindness and respect.

Societal structures and policies include dominant norms and stereotypes as well as structural factors that enhance or limit opportunities for individuals and groups. Societal biases and stereotypes can influence bullying dynamics in even the youngest of children, and therefore close consideration of this in the Canadian context is important. Since we know power imbalances are influential in bullying dynamics, it is no surprise that structural factors—which operate to enrich opportunities for some but not others—influence bullying behaviours among children and youth.

Finally, the *cyber world* includes social media tools and smart phones, which can impact child and youth development, and which can also influence prevention and intervention efforts. Chapter 2 provides extensive discussion of the cyber world and its relation to child development and bullying. It is important to reiterate here that the cyber world influences and is influenced by all other levels of the ecological system.[4]

An expanded ecological systems framework can be used as a way to map out possible interventions in bullying situations. Using this perspective, the complexity of bullying incidents is taken into account so that we recognize the multiple levels at which we can prevent and intervene. Courtney, Edward, Sarah, Kevin, Laura, and Shayne all live in complex worlds that include their families, friends and peers, classrooms, schools, communities, and societies—and, more recently, the cyber world. Factors at each of these levels influence bullying dynamics and help or hinder intervention strategies. In the example of *Courtney*, as several students in the class are playing the "Queen Suzie" game, it might be best to intervene at the classroom level, attending to both the larger school environment and the individual children in the class—for example, the girl and boy who are queen and king and the others who go along with this. For *Edward* (bias against new Canadians), *Shayne* (bias against sexual minorities), and *Laura* (bias against girls and women), bias and discrimination within the school and society as a whole contributed to their bullying situations. School-level interventions may assist in breaking these biases and promoting acceptance. For *Laura* (cyberbullying), individual and family counselling would be beneficial, in addition to a strong response from the school and potentially the police in order to address her ex-boyfriend's actions. For *Sarah* (bullied by her friends), some individual counselling with a school social worker or guidance counsellor might help her to talk about her distress and develop assertiveness. Education for teachers in her school may help them recognize all forms of bullying, even those that involve popular students who do well academically. Perhaps in the case of *Kevin* (invited to join an exclusionary club), intervention should occur at the school level in a way that targets parental actions, educates parents about exclusionary behaviour, and promotes healthy peer relations.

Conclusion

We must not confuse the pervasiveness of bullying with the assumption that it is easy to understand and address. Given its complexity, an ecological systems framework is the most suitable lens through which to understand the factors that contribute to bullying dynamics. We must recognize the complexity of these dynamics and avoid oversimplifying the resultant problems. Using this lens, we will be able to more effectively understand the "big picture" and at the same time identify where in the system to intervene and in what order to prevent and stop bullying.

Chapter 6

Prevention and Intervention

Introduction

Young people have the right to grow up feeling safe and secure, free from threat and victimization. Adults are obligated to make sure this is the case in all respects, and they have a legal duty to protect children and youth from bullying. As we discussed in previous chapters, bullying can take many forms, some more obvious than others; all, however, are serious. The consequences can be mild or severe, depending on a range of factors that include the characteristics of the child, the bullying situation, the family and neighbourhood, as well as the school and cultural context. We must work together toward the collective goal of bullying prevention. However, when it does take place, it is important that we intervene effectively, given how much is at stake. Children involved in bullying often have trouble at school, not to mention difficulty relating to their peers, among other issues. The effects of being a victim, perpetrator, or both can reverberate into adulthood. Bullying may contribute to mental health issues and even suicide among victims, and delinquent or criminal behaviour among aggressors. In this chapter, we briefly review existing anti-bullying initiatives and the evidence of their effectiveness. We also consider ways of combatting bullying in the absence of an explicit initiative. Finally, we provide an overview of the challenges in responding to bullying and offer guidelines for overcoming these.

Anti-bullying Initiatives

Experts agree that anti-bullying initiatives must take into account the multiple causes of bullying, and must also address the context in which it takes place. Initiatives cannot only focus on the individual bully or victim, but must direct themselves to the "bigger picture." A wide variety of anti-bullying initiatives exist: of these, some target the peer group; others the family or community; still others focus on the classroom, teachers, and school administrators. Some are aimed at the whole school, or a combination of groups. In this section, we highlight three distinct anti-bullying models: "whole-school" approaches, peer support models, and the restorative justice model.

Whole-school approaches

Children spend a great deal of time in school, learning the formal curriculum as well as the informal and implicit lessons that take place in daily interactions with peers, teachers, and other adults. Since children spend so much time at school, and bullying often occurs in this context, it makes sense for most anti-bullying initiatives to be based in the school. Dan Olweus (1991) developed the first whole-school anti-bullying program, which is now possibly the most well-known and widely evaluated program in the world.

The Olweus Bullying Prevention Programme has been rigorously evaluated and deemed to be effective in Norway and the United States. It has been shown to have a promising impact on bullying (Olweus 2004). The program targets the whole school, the classroom, the individual students and their parents, and the community. A Bullying Prevention Coordinating Committee is established to provide oversight to the program, and school staff participate in discussion groups. Emphasis is placed on reviewing and refining the current supervisory system at the school, and staff focus on implementing effective supervision for students during break times. At the same time, class rules against bullying are developed and enforced, and individual intervention plans are formed for children involved in bullying as bullies or victims. Sanctions for students who bully, for example, include holding serious talks with principals or teachers, sitting outside the principal's office, or staying close to the teacher during break times or recesses. Other program components include parent-teacher meetings to discuss bullying, and conversations with children not involved in bullying to encourage them to become effective helpers. Although this program was developed for schools, it can be adapted for use in any setting in which children and youth are in regular attendance, such as camps or youth programs. Hearing a consistent anti-bullying message across multiple settings is particularly helpful, emphasizing to young people that bullying is an issue that concerns the whole community.[1]

In the past decades following the seminal work of Dan Olweus, many other whole-school programs have been developed. The features of these programs vary, and they are often implemented differently across diverse school settings. Despite these variations, several commonalities exist among whole-school approaches. These programs typically aim to change the attitudes that underlie bullying behaviours and increase tolerance for differences. Parental involvement is considered critical, as are more targeted interventions for the children and youth involved in bullying. Many whole-school programs include an anti-bullying curriculum as a component. An advantage of curriculum programs is that they do not require a great deal of commitment in terms of resources, personnel, and effort. Moreover, teachers can interweave violence prevention concepts with topics such as self-esteem and conflict resolution, and can address issues as they emerge, in the moment.[2]

Peer support models

Peer support initiatives focus primarily on improving relations among students. Peer-led interventions typically entail teaching peer helpers the basic skills of active listening, empathy, problem solving, and support so that they can help other students who are involved in bullying. In some programs, youth are encouraged to provide support to victims of bullying, often formally as a "mentor" or "buddy." In other programs, the focus is on helping young people to act courageously and stand up for peers when they witness incidents of bullying. Leadership and conflict resolution may also be encouraged.

Peer-led approaches may be especially helpful for adolescents, who are typically less willing to accept adult authority and direction. Still, adult authority may be necessary to address bullying problems. The power imbalances that exist among peers often contribute to bullying situations, which is why it might be so difficult for young people to challenge power dynamics on their own. Adult involvement provides a certain level of authority that can help young people in shifting those power dynamics to become more balanced.[3]

Restorative justice approach

The restorative justice model is another approach for addressing bullying, which consists of restoring relationships through forgiveness and reconciliation. Central to this approach is the principle that young people involved in bullying should not lose their social ties and should not be stigmatized or humiliated in trying to "right" the "wrong" of bullying. The goal of restorative justice is to resolve conflict through promoting social responsibility and minimizing the stigma for the children involved in bullying. Typically the child or youth's natural network is gathered together to offer support. This natural network may include an individual's parents, aunts, uncles, and grandparents. This group is brought together with the school community and, if appropriate, the police. In an approach that involves restorative justice, a child or youth who bullies has the opportunity to take responsibility for his or her actions, to make amends with the victim, and to reintegrate into their peer group. Those who have been victimized are able to express the harm they have experienced in an environment in which they are valued and respected. It takes a great deal of emotional courage for bullies to admit what they have done and for victims to forgive and agree to move forward constructively. A "safe space" is required in which both bullies and victims feel respected and supported, and in which both are willing to find a way forward to address the consequences and harms of the bullying experience.[4]

Restorative justice is believed to help a child or youth behave adaptively in future relationships. The restorative justice approach is often considered more progressive than punitive approaches to bullying, although controversy surrounds this issue. Several experts in the field assert that "zero tolerance"-style approaches, such as expelling students who bully or placing them with other reprimanded youngsters, are exclusionary and fail to provide the offending students with opportunities to develop positive social and relationship skills (Pepler, Smith, & Rigby 2004). Others believe that rules against bullying are necessary, and that specific consequences must be in place should these rules be broken. The debate is ongoing, although evidence suggests that both sides may be right, and that punitive and non-punitive approaches can be combined (Ttofi & Farrington 2012). We will expand on this topic later.

Effectiveness of Anti-bullying Initiatives

There is no shortage of anti-bullying prevention and intervention programs. There is, however, a shortage of programs with known effectiveness; research findings on bullying programs tend to be mixed and inconclusive. Some studies show positive albeit modest effects of interventions, while other studies report few positive changes; in some cases, studies have even noted negative effects.[5] These mixed findings are likely a result of differences in the research methods used as well as differences among the children, youth, teachers, and schools that participated in the studies. Existing research has involved participants of a variety of ages and from a variety of locations throughout the world. A spectrum of analytic techniques has been used to analyze data from these participants—some techniques more sophisticated than others.

There are many publications on anti-bullying programs across the world. It can be daunting to evaluate this huge body of research. Study findings can be confusing, and few of us have the ability to critically assess the value of the results. Some studies may suggest that a specific anti-bullying program is very effective, but it takes years of training and experience to know how much weight to give these findings. How did the researchers recruit the sample of participants? What research design was used? Was bullying assessed in numerous different ways, at numerous time points? Were qualitative research methods used in conjunction with quantitative methods to enhance the research design? If statistical analyses were conducted, did the researchers control for the many factors that can influence bullying, other than the anti-bullying program in question? To help us interpret large bodies of research, some scholars have produced systematic reviews and meta-analyses, which are particularly useful when trying to understand the effectiveness of anti-bullying initiatives.

A *systematic review* is essentially a summary of existing research. However, it differs from a standard literature review in important ways. The term "systematic review" implies that the process of collecting, reviewing, and presenting evidence on a certain topic is standardized and therefore can be replicated. All evidence on a particular topic that fits pre-specified eligibility criteria is reviewed and collated using transparent and systematic methods in order to minimize bias. A *meta-analysis* occurs after a review of the literature is completed. Scholars extract data from the articles that they have reviewed, and then pool all these data to create an overall summary of the findings.[6]

Several systematic reviews and meta-analyses have been conducted that focus on bullying prevention and intervention programs. In 2007, Christopher Ferguson and his colleagues conducted a meta-analytic review of 42 published studies on the effectiveness of school-based anti-bullying programs. One scholarly database was searched for all articles published between 1995 and 2006 that focused on a bullying intervention with random assignment to an experimental and a control group to test program effectiveness. This means that researchers in these studies randomly assigned students, classrooms, or schools to receive the intervention, comprising an "experimental group." Other students, classrooms, or schools were randomly assigned to the "control group," or in other words, the group that did not receive the intervention. The use of random assignment in experimental research is generally considered to be a marker for a high-quality study. The findings of this meta-analysis suggest that the anti-bullying programs produced a small amount of positive change, but that this change was not large enough to be practically significant.

Maria Ttofi and David Farrington of the United Kingdom conducted a systematic review and meta-analysis of intervention research published from 1983 to 2008, widely recognized to be the most comprehensive and rigorous review and analysis to date (Ttofi & Farrington 2009). Both their search of the literature and analysis of data from individual studies were extensive. They only included studies that compared those students who received an intervention (an experimental group) with those who did not (a control group), and ones that involved 200 or more students. In total, reports on 30 anti-bullying programs were included in this review. Overall, the programs reviewed had a substantial effect on bullying, reducing bullying by 23 percent and victimization by 20 percent. This means that across the various programs, there were approximately 23 percent fewer bullies in the experimental groups (i.e., the groups that received the programs) compared to the control groups (i.e., the groups that did not receive the programs). Likewise, there were about 20 percent fewer victims in the experimental groups compared to the control groups.

To investigate the specific elements of these programs that were most helpful, Ttofi and Farrington contacted the original evaluators to obtain more detailed information on the programs. The program elements they examined included:

- Whole-school anti-bullying policies
- Classroom rules
- School conferences providing information on bullying to students
- Curriculum materials
- Classroom management
- Co-operative group work among teachers or counsellors
- Work with bullies and victims
- Work with peers
- Information for teachers and parents
- Improved playground supervision
- Disciplinary methods
- Restorative justice approaches
- School tribunals and bully courts
- Teacher and parent training
- Videos and virtual reality computer games

They also noted the extent to which the program was inspired by the work of Dan Olweus by assessing how similar each program was to the Olweus Bullying Prevention Programme. In addition, the length (i.e., number of days) and level of intensity (i.e., number of hours teachers and children participated) of each program was noted. The analysis revealed that the most effective programs involved training and information for parents, improved playground supervision, disciplinary methods (e.g., talk with the principal), school conferences, and classroom rules and management. Overall, programs that built in more elements, were longer in duration and more intense, and were inspired by Olweus appeared to be most effective in reducing bullying. Generally, the programs were more effective with older children, and more effective when implemented in Europe, and Norway in particular. Ttofi and Farrington suggest that perhaps programs implemented in Norway and Europe more generally were more effective because of the long tradition of bullying research and programming in Scandinavian countries, of course beginning with the work of Dan Olweus. It is also important to remember that there are vast differences between Europe and North America, which most likely affect the implementation and success of anti-bullying initiatives. Consider, for instance, the differences in population, history, culture, social norms, family practices, and education and other social policies. Some scholars hypothesize that the success of anti-bullying initiatives in Scandinavia can be attributed to the higher-quality schools, smaller class sizes, and better-trained teachers in this region (see Smith et al. 2004). Others believe that anti-bullying programs like Olweus's are simply not as effective when implemented in diverse nations like Canada and the United States. Olweus disagrees, noting that one city (Oslo, Norway) in which his program was successful is quite diverse, and that results from studies evaluating his program in the United States are promising (Olweus & Limber 2010b).

Since Ttofi and Farrington published their first systematic review and meta-analysis, they have continued their work, updating their review and conducting more specific analyses (Ttofi & Farrington 2011, 2012). Based on the updates, they concluded that the interventions were associated with a 20–23 percent decrease in bullying and a 17–20 percent decrease in victimization. In addition to the elements found to be most effective in the previous review, their updated work found three separate elements effective in reducing bullying: teacher training, whole-school anti-bullying policies, and co-operative group work. One program element—work with peers—was associated with an increase in victimization.

Following questions from other scholars about some of these findings (see Smith, Salmivalli, & Cowie, 2012), Ttofi and Farrington delved deeper into their analyses to focus on three of their more contentious findings: (1) the association between work with peers and increased victimization; (2) the association between disciplinary methods and a reduction in bullying and victimization; and (3) the finding that programs are more effective with older students.

With regards to the first finding, Ttofi and Farrington present convincing evidence that programs focusing on work with peers—defined as peer mediation, peer mentoring, or engagement of bystanders in bullying situations—have not been effective in reducing bullying and victimization. They suggest that this may be due to the significant challenges such programs face. There may be limited support and commitment for these programs from school staff and students, and those students who act as supporters or mentors may not know effective ways of intervening in bullying situations. For instance, peer supporters may intervene in an aggressive fashion, which only serves to reciprocate aggression and in turn worsen relationships among students. Other scholars have also criticized both the peer support and restorative justice models for failing to address the power imbalances that exist in bullying situations (Black et al. 2010).

In terms of the positive effects associated with disciplinary methods, Ttofi and Farrington clarify that none of the programs involving so-called punitive disciplinary methods used a zero-tolerance approach. Rather, these disciplinary methods included serious talks with students, depriving students of some privileges—for example, the ability to play at recess—and other similar actions. In some programs, these methods were used in combination with non-punitive measures such as restorative justice. Ttofi and Farrington emphasize the importance of enforcing rules against bullying in a respectful, non-hostile, and non-stigmatizing way.

In contrast to the findings of Ttofi and Farrington, some researchers have found that bullying prevention programs are more effective for younger students. Ttofi and Farrington investigated the influence of age further by examining more studies, including some that were not incorporated into their previous reviews, and noted that they were left with conflicting findings. Even so, they emphasize that early intervention is important to stop bullying before it spirals out of control.

Joshua Polanin, Dorothy Espelage, and Therese Pigott (2012) conducted a meta-analysis to examine whether prevention programs increased the likelihood of young people standing up for a peer who is being bullied. These researchers searched five databases for studies published from 1980 to 2010 that focused on bystander behaviour as a primary outcome and that compared an experimental group to a control group. This search resulted in 11 studies for review, most of which were conducted in the United States and the remainder in Europe. The results of the meta-analysis suggest that the programs increased the likelihood that bystanders would intervene in bullying situations, but did not increase the likelihood that others would feel empathy for the victims. Few studies measured the impact of interventions on empathy, which may explain the lack of a significant finding in this regard. Interventions with high school students were more effective than those implemented with primary school students, suggesting that the developmental stage of young people may affect their ability to intervene in bullying situations. Other factors, such as program location (United States versus Europe), treatment length, and parental involvement did not appear to have an influence on bystander behaviour.

What Influences the Success of Anti-Bullying Initiatives?

The success of anti-bullying initiatives is dependent on a number of factors. School-based programs will likely be more successful if teachers, principals, and other staff are committed to ending bullying and are supportive of the anti-bullying initiative. All anti-bullying initiatives require some degree of financial support, either from governmental or other sources of funding (Pepler, Smith, & Rigby 2004; Whitted & Dupper 2005).

In some schools, a lack of support and funding for anti-bullying initiatives is the reality. It is very challenging to design studies that are both methodologically rigorous and representative of the reality for particular children, teachers, administrators, and school districts. It is important to remember that the controlled conditions under which experiments and other research studies are conducted can be very different from the actual conditions of a school or classroom. A program that is effective in decreasing bullying in a study might therefore not be effective in the real world (Black et al. 2010). For instance, participation in research studies is often voluntary. Those schools or teachers that voluntarily decide to implement a bullying program when asked by researchers likely differ in some ways from those that decline the invitation to participate. Perhaps those who volunteer believe bullying is an important problem that needs to be addressed, possibly because it has been identified in their school. Or perhaps these schools have the resources necessary to support an anti-bullying program. Teachers who opt not to participate might feel bullying is not a priority, or alternatively, they might feel overwhelmed with other responsibilities and thus unable to participate. In a real-world context, an "effective" program might be less effective in this school. Clearly, programs must be tailored to specific school contexts with feasibility in mind, and must be implemented and evaluated even in challenging and resource-limited school contexts.

Anti-bullying programs can be effective under some conditions and ineffective under others. For instance, although the Olweus Bullying Prevention Programme has worked well in reducing bullying in Scandinavia, it has been less successful in other countries (Pepler, Smith, & Rigby 2004). One possible reason for this is that the intervention may have been implemented differently across the various settings. Olweus discussed some of the challenges in implementing his Bullying Prevention Programme (Olweus 2004). Using data from a research evaluation of his program, Olweus and colleagues conducted complex statistical analyses to understand the factors that influenced the implementation of his intervention. They examined, for instance, whether teachers actually followed the program components, such as establishing class rules against bullying. They found that teachers who saw themselves as important in combatting bullying were more likely to take part in anti-bullying efforts. Those who viewed it as their responsibility and the responsibility of the school to counteract bullying were also more likely to take part in anti-bullying efforts. In addition, teachers who read the materials provided as part of the program were more likely to follow the components, likely because the materials inspired them to be more informed. These findings suggest that teachers play a critical role in the implementation of anti-bullying initiatives in schools.

Anti-bullying initiatives will likely be more successful if they are tailored to children and youth according to their age, developmental stage, gender, and capacities. Certain interventions may be more effective with younger children, whereas others might work better for older children. For instance, as children grow older, their understanding of bullying might become more complex. Interventions for older children might therefore be able to introduce more complex concepts than would be appropriate for younger children. Older children and youth might understand that bullying is a human rights issue, and that it is their right to feel safe and respected. They might also be more receptive to learning about power dynamics, societal stereotypes and biases, and conflict management and resolution. Younger children would likely be unable to understand these more advanced concepts (Pepler, Smith, & Rigby 2004).

Canadian Programs and Their Effectiveness

More research is needed to document the anti-bullying initiatives that are in place across Canada and to evaluate their effectiveness in reducing bullying. We have a limited understanding of what is being done to combat bullying in Canada and how well it is working. In this section, we describe several Canadian anti-bullying initiatives and their effectiveness.

The Dare to Care—Bully Proofing Your School program is a schoolwide comprehensive approach to bullying originally modelled after the Olweus Bullying Prevention Programme (Beran, Tutty, & Steinrath 2004). In this program, facilitators offer training and support to school personnel in the form of one full-day professional development workshop. In addition, students, parents, and school personnel collaborate to develop a discipline policy that defines bullying and the consequences for this behaviour.

Finally, teachers implement a classroom curriculum that includes education on bullying through techniques such as role-plays, videos, and skits. To assess the benefits of this program, 197 students in grades four to six in four Calgary elementary schools participated in an evaluation. Students in one school were tested before the program was introduced and then tested again three months later; students in another comparison school were tested during the same timelines but did not receive the intervention. Two additional schools were tested, one after the program had been implemented for one year and another after the program had been implemented for two years. All of the program components were implemented in the three "intervention" schools, but students in the one-year and two-year program schools had participated in more anti-bullying activities than students in the three-month program school. The results showed that the frequency of being bullied and the strategies used to help victims did not change between the time the intervention was introduced and the three-month follow-up in both the three-month program school and the comparison, no-intervention school. Even though the three "intervention" schools had experienced Dare to Care for varying amounts of time, there were few differences across the schools in terms of bullying outcomes, meaning that the two-year program school had similar outcomes to the three-month program school. Overall, the study provided limited support for the Dare to Care program.

Debra Pepler and her colleagues implemented and evaluated an anti-bullying initiative in three elementary schools in Toronto in the 1990s, based on Olweus's program (Pepler et al. 2004). This program was grounded in an understanding that bullying extends beyond the individual bullies and victims and is influenced by the whole school, the family, and the community. It was developed by Pepler and colleagues, and was informed by research they were conducting at the time. The program had several components, including staff training, developing codes of behaviour, improving playground supervision, and holding parent information nights. Children developed class rules, and activities were introduced to promote communication and peer support. Those children involved in bullying received more specific interventions, including parent contact and follow-up, and schools were encouraged to document the children involved in bullying and their responses to these issues.

Three schools were selected to take part in the program and the evaluation, based on the willingness of principals and teachers to participate. Two classes were randomly selected from each grade from grades one through six in each school, for a total of 36 classes. The schools varied in demographics of students and their families, but all reflected the diversity of Toronto to some degree. For instance, the percentage of students with a first language other than English ranged from 15 percent in one school to 70 percent in another school. In the final year of the study, there were 306 participating children in one school, 163 in the second school, and 289 in the third school. The program was evaluated from the perspectives of teachers, students, and parents, using both questionnaires and observational data.

Pepler and colleagues acknowledge the many challenges in implementing and evaluating the anti-bullying program. For instance, the implementation of the intervention varied across the schools, depending on the school principals and the school context. Nevertheless, the researchers obtained important feedback about implementing and evaluating anti-bullying initiatives in Canada. School personnel clearly play a key role in generating and maintaining interest and support for anti-bullying initiatives. By demonstrating commitment to an anti-bullying initiative, adults are not only validating the experiences of children who have been victimized, but also serve as fundamental role models for children and youth. This study also suggests that, for the best results, anti-bullying initiatives must be implemented in the long term. In the evaluation by Pepler and colleagues, it appears that little changed in the initial months of implementing the program, but significant improvements in bullying problems did appear in the longer term, after the program had been implemented from about 18 to 30 months. Even after two-and-a-half years of the program at one school, however, students were still not more likely to intervene when they saw peers experiencing bullying. This is a reminder that many factors influence the effectiveness of anti-bullying initiatives, including the school context.

Roots of Empathy (ROE; www.rootsofempathy.org) is a program that was developed by Mary Gordon in Canada for children from kindergarten to grade eight. The goals of the program include developing children's social and emotional understanding, promoting pro-social and inhibiting aggressive behaviours, and increasing children's knowledge of human development and responsive parenting. While not specifically aimed at bullying, ROE has been identified as an anti-bullying program due to its focus on aggression, empathy, and relationships. Bullying is an aggressive behaviour and a relationship problem, and the aim of the ROE program is to teach children to understand how others feel and take responsibility for their actions and inactions.

The ROE program is implemented for nine months, and includes each class "adopting" an infant and his or her parent(s) from the community. The infant and parent(s) visit monthly, allowing the children to learn about infant development and growth over time. A program instructor also visits the class to provide twice-monthly lessons designed to foster empathy, emotional understanding, and problem-solving skills. Teachers are expected to incorporate the ideas from the infant visits and the program instructor lessons into the general education program. For instance, teachers can use the infant visit as a platform from which to begin discussions of diversity in the classroom, noting that family configurations are variable and that this diversity should be celebrated. Throughout the school year, the infant visits and teacher instruction are meant to cultivate a culture of caring and respect, in which all children in the class learn to care both for the infant as well as for one another, and to respect the uniqueness of all individuals. ROE is strongly rooted in empirical as well as theoretical understandings of the factors that elicit both aggression and pro-social behaviours, such as attachment, temperament, and perspective taking.

Emerging research suggests that the ROE program can potentially lead to decreases in child aggression, including both physical and relational aggression. In one of the first studies to systematically examine the effectiveness of the ROE program, Kimberly Schonert-Reichl and colleagues compared 14 elementary schools in which ROE was implemented to the same number of elementary schools that did not implement ROE. The schools were located in Vancouver and Toronto, and a total of 585 children attending these schools participated in the study. Social and emotional competence was assessed both before and after the implementation of the program. The results indicated that children in the ROE program showed significant increases in pro-social behaviours and significant decreases in proactive and relational aggression (Roots of Empathy 2009; Schonert-Reichl et al. 2012).

In an attempt to document existing efforts to combat bullying in Canada, J.D. Smith and colleagues surveyed a random sample of school administrators in Ontario about the anti-bullying programs in place at their schools (Smith, Cousins, & Stewart 2005). From the perspectives of the administrators, the success of anti-bullying interventions hinged on two key factors: availability of resources and the amount of anti-bullying programming. Consistent with the research findings reported previously in this chapter, these administrators aptly noted that anti-bullying interventions were more successful when sufficient resources were available to implement them, and when the programs had multiple components. Not surprisingly, these factors were related. The amount of programming offered in schools increased with the level of available resources. For the administrators surveyed, the time, effort, and money invested in anti-bullying initiatives had a clear impact on actual bullying outcomes for the children in their schools. While this might seem obvious or apparent, these findings send a clear message to researchers, policy makers, and funding bodies. Multi-faceted and intensive anti-bullying programs are needed, and resources must be available to sufficiently support these programs.

Combatting Bullying Without an Explicit Anti-Bullying Initiative

A great deal of progress can be accomplished even in the absence of an explicit anti-bullying initiative. Ideally situated to address bullying, school-based practitioners can provide individual and group counselling for students and can meet with their parents and families. Practitioners include guidance counsellors, social workers, child and youth workers, psychologists, and other professionals. These practitioners can facilitate parent-school contact, foster communication and co-operation between parents and teachers, and refer children and families to community services. They are well situated to mediate between parents and the school, as well as help empower parents and defend the children's rights.[7]

All school personnel can work to combat bullying, including staff and administrators, lunch supervisors, and extracurricular leaders. It is important that these adults understand the complexities of bullying and recognize the detrimental effects of even apparently minor (and common) behaviours (see Elinoff, Chafouleas, & Sassu 2004). Typically, administrators are responsible for ensuring that adults are vigilant in supervising throughout the school and that transparent procedures are in place through which to report and respond to bullying. Administrators as well as teachers and other staff can promote a school culture and climate that encourages healthy relationships, inclusion, and a firm but non-hostile response to bullying situations.

Children and youth need help from adults to grow into confident individuals who are caring and empathic toward others and courageous enough to stand up to bullying in appropriate and non-aggressive ways. Adults can help children by promoting self-esteem, teaching and modelling positive conflict-resolution skills, and demonstrating for children how to maintain healthy relationships. This can go a long way in addressing bullying.

Challenges in Preventing, Assessing, and Intervening in Bullying

We conclude this chapter by discussing three key challenges that make it difficult to respond to bullying situations, and by providing guidelines to overcome these challenges. First, bullying is dynamic and always occurs in the context of the ecological system.[8] This makes it complex and changeable. It is important to recognize that we are always working with a "moving target." A child might shift fluidly and quickly from bully to victim to bystander. Some may never be involved in bullying during childhood, whereas others may be involved intermittently or chronically. A child who bullies may have poor social skills, or alternatively his or her social skills may be exceptional. A child who is victimized at school may also be victimized at home and in cyberspace. Assessing potential bullying situations requires that we take a close look at the characteristics of the children involved, as well as the environments in which these children grow up. Doing so can assist us in identifying potential factors exacerbating the bullying and allow us to determine the best response.

Secondly, it is challenging to not be swayed by the many myths that exist about bullying, which influence how we assess and understand particular situations. Wendy Craig, Debra Pepler, and Joanne Cummings (2013), leading experts on bullying in Canada, outlined six common myths about bullying in their handbook entitled "Bullying Prevention." First, it is commonly believed that children *grow out of bullying*. This is a myth. Bullying problems must be identified and addressed early in order to prevent patterns of aggression from becoming more established. Another myth is that *only a small number of children have problems with bullying*. This myth can lead educators and policy makers to assume that widespread prevention and intervention programs are unnecessary. It is important to recognize that many children are involved in bullying at some point, and even those who are not directly involved may witness bullying. This can be distressing. Some children, and even adults, believe that *reporting bullying will only make it worse*. As Craig and colleagues note, silence only empowers those who bully, deepening the power imbalance that often exists in bullying situations. Telling others about bullying *is* helpful in ending the victimization. At times, children are encouraged to *stand up and fight back in the face of victimization*. This is not a helpful suggestion for children, and can actually make the interaction worse. While assertiveness is a useful trait in bullying situations, it is always better for children to tell an adult about being victimized rather than respond with aggression. Another common myth is that bullying is a *school problem*; in actuality, bullying occurs anywhere that children come together to interact, including the neighbourhood or community, social settings such as sports teams, and of course the cyber world. Finally, it is commonly thought that *bullying does not occur within families*. As discussed in Chapter 4, bullying can indeed occur among siblings, and the family is the first context in which children experience and learn about relationships.

Finally, in order to intervene in a bullying situation we must know that it is taking place. Although bullying at times occurs in the presence of adults, more often adults are not around. Even when it takes place right under an adult's nose, it can be difficult to detect. A serious concern is that young people often do not tell adults about their victimization. And then when they do tell, adults sometimes do not take their reports about victimization seriously. This can decrease the likelihood that children and youth will talk to adults about bullying in the future. It is also likely to increase their distress.

Guidelines to Address Challenges

1. Accept that bullying is complex and confusing to recognize, define, and name. It will be complicated to wade through the myths that abound about bullying—and even more so, at times it will be difficult to decide what to do in the face of bullying. It is okay to be confused. Oversimplifying any bullying situation will not be helpful.
2. Carefully consider the factors at all levels of the ecological context that might be influencing the situation. This can help to determine where to intervene.
3. Try to answer a few questions to shed light on the situation:
   - What do the children involved think of the situation?
   - Is the situation causing distress for the children directly involved and those who witness it?
   - Do any children or youth need to speak with a counsellor, social worker, or other professional, either immediately or in the long term?
   - Has anyone tried to resolve the situation?
   - What is the relationship among the children involved?
   - Does the incident match your definition of bullying?
   - Do teachers, parents, and other adults see it as bullying?
   - Is anyone blaming the victim?
   - Do others think the bullying behaviour is normal or "not that bad?"
4. Remember that adults can make a big difference. Despite the complexities, it is possible to assess bullying situations, understand the dynamics at play, and intervene where appropriate. Not only is it possible, it is necessary. Adults are obligated to protect the rights of children and youth; bullying must not be ignored. It is important to keep in mind that adults intervening can help bring bullying to an end, alleviate distress for victimized children, and repair relational patterns for the involved children.
5. Look for signs of bullying. Be aware and mindful, and remember that many children and youth do not voluntarily tell adults about their victimization experiences. In a careful and thoughtful way, probe for further information if a child or youth begins to avoid school or certain social situations, suddenly stops spending time with certain friends, or appears to be distressed or physically hurt.
6. Once we are aware of a bullying incident, we must listen, understand, and validate the *subjective* experiences of the children involved, regardless of how others view the situation. It is crucial that adults listen to

children with a non-judgmental stance in order to encourage young people to talk about their experiences and to ask for help from adults before the bullying and the child's distress escalate.

7. Be empathic. Victims of bullying deserve and need empathy, and it is important to recognize the impact of all forms of bullying on them, even if the incident does not appear to be a "big deal."

Conclusions

It is clear that we cannot simply ignore bullying or dismiss it as a normal part of growing up. We must work to prevent bullying, and we must also intervene in situations where it is not prevented. Many anti-bullying initiatives have been developed, but research findings are mixed. We do know that anti-bullying efforts must take into account the multiple causes and effects of bullying, and also address the context in which it takes place. In general, interventions that are comprehensive and intensive will have a better chance at reducing bullying and victimization. Schools are ideal locations to implement anti-bullying programs, but all settings in which children spend time should consider working against bullying, either through formal initiatives or informal practices such as education about healthy relationships and sanctions for aggression. Olweus's Bullying Prevention Programme clearly shows promise in addressing bullying in Europe, although evaluations are less consistent when the program is implemented in North America. We need more research in Canada to determine which anti-bullying interventions are most effective for the children and youth in our diverse nation. Several challenges exist in tackling bullying in Canada and elsewhere, but these can be addressed with a strong commitment to preventing bullying for all children and youth.

Notes

Chapter 1

1. See, for example, Atlas & Pepler 1998; Finkelhor 1995; Olweus 1991, 1997.
2. On toleration of bullying and its pervasiveness, see Smith & Brain 2000. On its normalization, see Carter & Spencer 2006. On recognition of bullying as a public health issue, see Blosnich & Bossarte 2011.
3. For more details of Olweus's work, see Olweus 1988, 1991, 1992, 1994; Olweus & Limber 2010a; Olweus, Limber, & Mihalic 2000.
4. On policies, see Cassidy, Jackson, & Brown 2009. On media attention, see Hinduja & Patchin 2010.
5. On definitions, see Smith et al. 2002; Finkelhor, Turner, & Hamby 2012; Vaillancourt et al. 2008.
6. On damage caused by aggression, see Craig, Pepler, & Blais 2007. On direct and indirect forms, see Crick & Grotpeter 1995; Cullerton-Sen & Crick 2005; Herrenkohl et al. 2007.
7. On relational aggression, see Crick 1996; Crick & Grotpeter 1996; Crick, Casas, & Ku 1999; Owens, Shute, & Slee 2000; Pellegrini & Roseth 2006. On reputational aggression, see Prinstein & Cillessen 2003. On psychological bullying, see Brendtro 2001; Goldstein & Tisak 2004; Scheithauer et al. 2006.
8. On overlooking damage, see Bauman & Del Rio 2006; Craig, Pepler, & Atlas 2000; Townsend-Wiggins 2001. On teachers ignoring bullying, see Brendtro 2001.
9. See Mishna, Pepler, & Wiener 2006; Mishna et al. 2005.
10. For details of the study see Mishna 2004; Mishna & Alaggia 2005; Mishna et al. 2005; Mishna, Pepler, & Wiener 2006; Mishna, Wiener, & Pepler 2008. Results of this study have also been published in Mishna 2012.
11. Pepler, Connolly, & Craig 1993, adapted from Olweus 1989.
12. On intentions, see Guerin & Hennessy 2002; Olweus 2013.
13. See Craig, Pepler, & Blais 2007; Espelage & Swearer 2003; Finkelhor, Turner, & Hamby 2012; Hinduja & Patchin 2009; Olweus 1991; Olweus 1993; Olweus 2013.
14. On importance of repetition, see Craig & Pepler 2007; Olweus 2013. On the limits of focusing on repetition, see Monks & Smith 2006; Olweus 1993.
15. On the effects of repetitive bullying, including fear, see Hazler et al. 2001; Lee 2006; Siann, Callaghan, Lockhart, & Rawson 1993.
16. On gender differences, see Brendtro 2001, Crick & Grotpeter 1995; Currie, Kelly, & Pomerantz 2007; Goldstein & Tisak 2004; Owens, Shute, & Slee 2000; Underwood, Galen, & Paquette 2001.
17. See, for example, Arslan et al. 2012; Harel-Fisch et al. 2011; Martinelli et al. 2011; Ramya & Kulkarni 2011.
18. On varying prevalence estimates, see Craig, Pepler, & Atlas 2000; Craig & Harel 2004; Smith et al. 2002. On methodology, see Crick & Grotpeter 1995; Olweus 2013.
19. On the National Longitudinal Survey of Children and Youth, see Beran 2008. For the Ontario study, see Vaillancourt et al. 2010. For the Western Canada study, see Hymel, Rocke-Henderson, & Bonanno 2005. For the Toronto observational study, see Atlas & Pepler 1998; Craig, Pepler, & Atlas 2000. For the Toronto longitudinal study, see Pepler et al. 2008. For the Canadian Council on Social Development report, see CCSD 2006.

20. On not telling adults, see deLara 2012; Mishna & Alaggia 2005; Mishna, Pepler, & Wiener 2006; Mishna, Cook, et al. 2010; Oliver & Candappa 2007; Pepler et al. 1994. On telling friends, see Hawkins & Craig 2001. On disclosure among marginalized young people, see Mishna, Newman, et al. 2009; Williams et al. 2005.

21. On the Canadian HBSC findings, see Craig et al. 2009. For UNICEF reports, see UNICEF 2007; UNICEF 2013a. On international comparisons, see Pepler & Craig 2011.

22. On leadership in Canada, see Mishna, Pepler, et al. 2010. On PREVNet, see Pepler & Craig 2011. For the parliamentary review on bullying, see Andreychuk & Fraser 2007. For the parliamentary review on cyberbullying, see Jaffer & Brazeau 2012.

23. On the impact of bullying, see Copeland et al. 2013; Olweus 1984; Rigby 2000; Schwartz et al. 2006. On internalizing/externalizing problems, see Olweus 1994; Ttofi et al. 2011a, 2011b.

24. On problems associated with victimization, see Beaty & Alexeyev 2008; Due et al. 2005; Hawker & Boulton 2000; Klomek, Sourander, & Gould 2010; Patchin & Hinduja 2010; Rigby 2000; Roland 2002; Williams et al. 1996.

25. On damage to sense of self, see Currie et al. 2007. For other effects of relational bullying see Bauman & Del Rio 2006; Crick, Grotpeter & Bigbee 2002; Owens, Shute, & Slee 2000. On gender differences, see Goldstein & Tisak 2004. On the cycle of bullying, see Crick & Bigbee 1998.

26. On the academic impact of bullying, see Beran & Lupart 2009; Beran, Hughes, & Lupart 2008; Clarke & Kiselica 1997; Harel-Fisch et al. 2011; Konishi et al. 2010; Rigby 2003; Vaillancourt et al. 2010.

27. On academic effects, see Nansel et al. 2001. On mental health issues, see Klomek et al. 2010; Kumpulainen, Räsänen, & Puura 2001; Slee 1995. On substance use, see Pepler 2006. For the progression of bullying, see Copeland et al. 2013; O'Connell, Pepler, & Craig 1999; Ttofi et al. 2011a.

Chapter 2

1. Several terms are used to describe cyberbullying, including electronic bullying, cyber aggression, and online bullying.

2. See, for example, Beran et al., forthcoming; Campbell et al. 2012; Macháčková et al. 2013; Smith 2012.

3. On definitions and issues, see Bauman 2009; Collier 2012; Patchin & Hinduja 2012; Smith, del Barrio, & Tokunaga 2013; Wade & Beran 2011; Ybarra & Mitchell 2004.

4. On repetition and observers, see Campbell 2005; Kowalski & Limber 2007; Slonje & Smith 2008; Wolak, Mitchell, & Finkelhor 2007. On power imbalance, see Olweus 2013.

5. On distinctions between traditional and cyberbullying, see Kowalski, Morgan, & Limber 2012; Mishna, McLuckie, & Saini 2009; Ng 2012.

6. On youth having grown up with and thus only knowing the digital world, see Prensky 2001; Valcke et al. 2010. On the pervasiveness of technology use, see Cassidy et al. 2009; Rideout, Foehr, & Roberts 2010.

7. On the use of technology by children and youth, see Hinduja & Patchin 2009; Mesch 2006; Livingstone 2007; Livingstone & Bober 2004.

8. On the benefits of cyber world, see Bauman 2009; Blais et al. 2008; Blumenfeld & Cooper 2010; Elwell, Grogan, & Coulson 2010; Jackson et al. 2006; Strom & Strom 2012; Strom et al. 2009; Valkenburg & Peter 2007a; Wolak, Mitchell, & Finkelhor

2003. On the risks of cyber world, see Gasser, Maclay, & Palfrey 2010; Livingstone & Haddon 2009.

9. On lack of cues, see Ang & Goh 2010. On anonymity and inhibition, see Hinduja & Patchin 2009.

10. For our research, see Mishna, Cook, et al. 2010.

11. On prevalence, see Kowalski et al. 2014.

12. For higher prevalence estimates, see Juvonen & Gross 2008; Mishna, Cook, et al. 2010; Raskauskas & Stoltz 2007. Preliminary results from our current three-year longitudinal study suggest a lower prevalence of cyberbullying.

13. On overlap, see Hinduja & Patchin 2008; Juvonen & Gross 2008; Li 2007; Raskauskas & Stoltz 2007; Schneider et al. 2012; Smith 2012; Willard 2010. On traditional bully-victims, see Khoury-Kassabri 2009; Haynie et al. 2001. On cyber bully-victims, see Mishna, Cook, et al. 2010; Law et al. 2012.

14. On the relationship context of cyberbullying, see Craig & Pepler 2007; Hinduja & Patchin 2008, 2009; Mishna, Saini, & Solomon 2009; Valkenburg & Peter 2007b. On witnesses, see Atlas & Pepler 1998; Choi & Cho 2012; Craig & Pepler 2007; Macháčková et al. 2013; Mishna, Cook, et al. 2010; Patchin & Hinduja 2006; Sbarbaro & Smith 2011. On positive and negative bystander behaviour, see Barlińska, Szuster, & Winiewski 2013.

15. See Agatston, Kowalski, & Limber 2007; Ang & Goh 2010; Aricak et al. 2008; Dehue, Bolman, & Vollink 2008; Pornari & Wood 2010.

16. For our research, see Mishna, Cook, et al. 2010; Mishna, McLuckie, & Saini 2009; Mishna et al. 2012. For other studies, see Guerra, Williamson, & Sadek 2012; Mitchell, Finkelhor, & Wolak 2007.

17. On the effects of cyberbullying, see Ang & Goh 2010; Beran & Li 2005; Campbell et al. 2012; Dehue et al. 2008; Juvonen & Gross 2008; Litwiller & Brausch 2013; Mitchell, Ybarra, & Finkelhor 2007; Modecki, Barber, & Vernon 2013; Ybarra, Diener-West, & Leaf 2007. On effects over and above traditional bullying, see Blais 2008; Bonanno & Hymel 2013; Brown, Jackson, & Cassidy 2006; Campbell 2005; Dooley, Pyzalski, & Cross 2009; Kowalski, Limber, & Agatston 2008; Slonje & Smith 2008.

18. On disclosure, see Agatston, Kowalski, & Limber 2007; Aricak et al. 2008; Cassidy, Jackson, & Brown 2009; Suniti Bhat 2008.

19. On responding to cyberbullying, see Brown, Jackson, & Cassidy 2006; Campbell 2013; Cross & Walker 2013; Walker 2012; Young n.d.

20. On suicide, see Cover 2012; Cash & Bridge 2009.

21. On these questions, see Auerbach 2009; Butler et al. 2011; Collier 2012; Dickerson 2009; Goodno 2007; Heidlage 2009; Ruedy 2008; Shariff & Hoff 2007.

22. On schools, see Beale & Hall 2007; Cassidy, Jackson, & Brown 2009; Mishna, Cook, et al. 2010.

23. See, e.g., *R. v. M.(A.)* [2008] SCC 19.

24. See Education Act, R.S.O., c E.2, ss. 1.0.0.2, 169(1)(a)(2), 301(6–7.1), 306.

25. See Education Act, SA 2012, c E-0.3, s.1(1)(d) (awaiting proclamation).

26. See Education Act, SA 2012, c E-0.3, s. 31(e).

27. See The Public Schools Act, C.C.S.M. c. P250, s. 1.2(2) (2013).

28. See Education Act, S.N.W.T. 1995, c. 28.

29. See Education Act, S.N.B. 1997, c. E-1.12.

30. See Education Act, SNS 1995–96, c 1, s. 122, as amended by Cyber-Safety Act, SNS 2013, c 2, s. 26.

31. See Criminal Code, RSC 1985, c C-46, ss. 264, 264.1.

32. Bill C-13, An Act to amend the Criminal Code, the Canada Evidence Act, the Competition Act and the Mutual Legal Assistance in Criminal Matters Act, 2nd Sess, 40th Parl, 2013 (first reading 20 November 2013).
33. See *R. v. Lucas* [1998] 1 S.C.R. 439.
34. See Cyber-Safety Act, SNS 2013, c 2.
35. See Cyber-Safety Act, SNS 2013, c 2, s. 22(3).
36. See Canadian Human Rights Act, R.S.C. 1985, c. H-6, s. 3.
37. *ibid.*, s. 13(1).
38. See *North Vancouver School District No. 44 v. Jubran* 2005 CarswellBC 788.

Chapter 3

1. On bias-based bullying, see Greene 2006; Rigby 2002; Stein 2003.
2. On diversification, see Dowden & Brennan 2012. On ethno-cultural and religious diversity and foreign-born populations, see Statistics Canada 2013. On families, see Milan, Vezina, & Wells 2007; Statistics Canada 2012. On disabilities, see Kowalchuk & Crompton 2009; Statistics Canada 2007.
3. See Griffith & Labercane 1995. For the study of North American youth on reserve, see Sittner Hartshorn, Whitbeck, & Hoyt 2012.
4. On the longitudinal study, see Pepler, Connolly, & Craig 1999; McKenney et al. 2006. On HBSC, see Larochette, Murphy, & Craig 2010. On First Nations youth, see Lemstra et al. 2011.
5. For details of the study see Mishna 2004; Mishna & Alaggia 2005; Mishna, Pepler, & Wiener 2006; Mishna et al. 2005; Mishna, Wiener, & Pepler 2008.
6. For mixed results from the United States, see Goldweber, Waasdorp, & Bradshaw 2013; Nansel et al. 2001; Stein, Dukes, & Warren 2007. On not calling it bullying, see Siann et al. 1994.
7. On definitions and pervasiveness of sexual harassment and sexualized bullying, see American Association of University Women Educational Foundation 1993, 2001; Dupper & Meyer-Adams 2002; Fineran & Bolen 2006; Land 2003; Nansel et al. 2001; Stein 1995, 1999; Timmerman 2003; Wise & Stanley 1987. On the lack of distinction between sexual harassment and sexual bullying, see N. Duncan 1999. On gender differences, see Chiodo et al. 2009; McMaster et al. 2002. On poor responses, see Rodkin & Fischer 2003; Stein 1995; Stone & Couch 2002; Timmerman 2003.
8. On labelling behaviour and education, see Rahimi & Liston 2011; Stein 1995.
9. On the pervasiveness of prejudice and bullying based on sexual orientation and gender identity, see Elze 2003; Kosciw, Bartkiewicz, & Greytak 2012; Meyer 2003; Pilkington & D'Augelli 1995; Poteat & Espelage 2005; Saewyc et al. 2007; Saewyc 2008; Schrader & Wells 2005; Taylor & Peter 2011; Telljohann & Price 1993; Williams et al. 2003, 2005. On consequences, see Russell et al. 2012; Poteat & Espelage 2007.
10. On elementary, high school, and university settings, see Janoff 2005; Robin et al. 2002; Solomon 2004; Thurlow 2001; Williams et al. 2005. On comments and labels, see Daley et al. 2008; Mishna et al. 2009; Poteat & Espelage 2005. On school culture, see Chesir-Teran 2003.
11. See Canadian Council on Social Development (CCSD) 2003; Davis, Howell, & Cooke 2002 (on stuttering); Dawkins 1996; Hugh-Jones & Smith 1999 (also on stuttering); Little 2002 (on Asperger syndrome); Norwich & Kelly 2004; Singer 2005 (on dyslexia); Thompson, Whitney, & Smith 1994 (on learning disabilities); Whitney, Smith,

& Thompson 1994 (on learning disabilities); Yude, Goodman, & McConachie 1998 (on hemiplegia).

12. On bullying and cerebral palsy, see Lindsay & McPherson 2012. On bullying and autism spectrum disorder, see Cappadocia, Weiss, & Pepler 2012.

13. On intersectionality, see Bogard 1999; Daley et al. 2008; Felix & McMahon 2006.

14. Section 15(1), see http://laws.justice.gc.ca/en/charter.

15. See http://laws-lois.justice.gc.ca/eng/acts/h-6/index.html.

16. *North Vancouver School District No. 44 v. Jubran* 2005 CarswellBC 788 British Columbia Court of Appeal.

17. On detrimental effects, see Nansel et al. 2001; O'Connell et al. 1999; Wessler & De Andrade 2006. On toxic environments, see Ryan & Rivers 2003.

18. On content of aggressive behaviour and language, see Fineran & Bolen 2006; Greene 2006; Kimmel & Mahler 2003; Poteat & Espelage 2007; Stein 1995; Wessler & De Andrade 2006.

Chapter 4

1. All examples are composites with no identifying information.

2. On relationships, see Berndt & Hoyle 1985; Crick & Nelson 2002; Sullivan 1953; Nangle et al. 2003.

3. On "drama," see Boyd & Marwick 2011.

4. The metaphor of scaffolding was introduced by Bruner 1971 and Vygotsky 1986.

5. On bullying and friends, see Champion, Vernberg, & Shipman 2003; Hodges et al. 1999; Juvonen & Galvan 2008; O'Connell, Pepler, & Craig 1999; Newcomb & Bagwell 1995; Sainio et al. 2011; Salmivalli 1999; Stevens, Van Oost, & De Bourdeaudhuij 2000.

6. See Mishna 2004; Mishna & Alaggia 2005; Mishna et al. 2005; Mishna, Pepler, & Wiener 2006; Mishna, Wiener, & Pepler 2008.

7. On siblings, see R.D. Duncan 1999; Ensor et al. 2010; Menesini, Camodeca, & Nocentini 2010. On the high rate of sibling bullying, see Lewit & Baker 1996; Skinner & Kowalski 2013. On its negative impact, see Tucker et al. 2013.

8. On families, see Menesini et al. 2010; Updegraff et al. 2005.

9. On the relation between sibling and peer bullying, see Menesini et al. 2010.

Chapter 5

1. Bill C-13, An Act to amend the Criminal Code, the Canada Evidence Act, the Competition Act and the Mutual Legal Assistance in Criminal Matters Act, 2nd Sess, 40th Parl, 2013 (first reading 20 November 2013).

2. On the cyber world and child development, see Johnson & Puplampu 2008; Johnson 2010. On the cyber world and the ecology of the child, see Martin & Stuart 2011. On the cyber world and child sexual abuse, see Martin 2010; Martin 2013; Martin & Alaggia 2013.

3. For full discussion of cyberbullying, see Chapter 2.

4. For original ecological systems theory, see Bronfenbrenner 1979; Bronfenbrenner 1994. For adaptation of ecological systems theory to reflect the technological revolution, see Johnson & Puplampu 2008; Johnson 2010; Martin 2013; Martin & Alaggia 2013.

Chapter 6

1. See www.violencepreventionworks.org/public/olweus_scope.page for more information.
2. On whole-school programs, see Marini & Dane 2008; Smith, Cousins, & Stewart 2005; Tutty 2002; Tutty et al. 2005; Vreeman & Carroll 2007.
3. On peer support models, see Englander & Lawson 2007; Menesini et al. 2003; Pepler, Smith, & Rigby 2004; Smith, Cousins, & Stewart 2005; Ttofi & Farrington 2012.
4. On restorative justice, see Ahmed & Braithwaite 2006, 2012.
5. On mixed findings, see Cowie et al. 2008; Farrington et al. 2008; Kärnä et al. 2011; Pepler et al. 2004.
6. For more information, see The Cochrane Collaboration (www.cochrane.org/cochrane -reviews) and The Campbell Collaboration (www.campbellcollaboration.org).
7. See Agresta 2004; Allen & Tracy 2004; Drolet, Paquin, & Soutyrine 2006; Dupper 2003.
8. See Chapter 5 for a discussion of the ecological context.

References

"10 Years Later, 'Star Wars Kid' Speaks Out." 2013. *Macleans*, 9 May. Accessed 1 February 2014. www2.macleans.ca/2013/05/09/10-years-later-the-star-wars-kid-speaks-out/.

Agatston, P.W., R. Kowalski, & S. Limber. 2007. "Students' Perspectives on Cyber Bullying." *Journal of Adolescent Health* 41: S59–S60.

Agresta, J. 2004. "Professional Role Perceptions of School Social Workers, Psychologists, and Counselors." *Children and Schools* 26 (3): 151–63.

Ahmed, E., & V. Braithwaite. 2006. "Forgiveness, Reconciliation, and Shame: Three Key Variables in Reducing School Bullying." *Journal of Social Issues* 62 (2): 347–70.

———. 2012. "Learning to Manage Shame in School Bullying: Lessons for Restorative Justice Interventions." *Critical Criminology* 20: 79–97.

Allen, S.F. & E.M. Tracy. 2004. "Revitalizing the Role of Home Visiting by School Social Workers." *Children & Schools* 26 (4): 197–208.

American Association of University Women Educational Foundation. 1993. *Hostile Hallways: The AAUW Survey on Sexual Harassment in America's Schools* (Research Report No. 923012). Washington, DC: Harris/Scholastic Research.

———. 2001. *Hostile Hallways: Bullying, Teasing and Sexual Harassment in School.* Washington, DC: Authorhouse.

Andreychuk, The Honourable R., & The Honourable J. Fraser. 2007. "The Silenced Citizens. Effective Implementation of Canada's International Obligations with Respect to the Rights of Children." Final Report of the Standing Senate Committee on Human Rights. Ottawa, ON: Government of Canada.

Ang, R.P., & D.H. Goh. 2010. "Cyberbullying among Adolescents: The Role of Affective and Cognitive Empathy, and Gender." *Child Psychiatry and Human Development* 41: 387–97.

Aricak, T., S. Siyahhan, A. Uzunhasanoglu, S. Saribeyoglu, S. Ciplak, N. Yilmaz, et al. 2008. "Cyberbullying among Turkish Adolescents." *Cyberpsychology & Behaviour* 11 (3): 253–63.

Arslan, S., V. Hallett, E. Akkas, & O.A. Akkas. 2012. "Bullying and Victimization among Turkish Children and Adolescents: Examining Prevalence and Associated Health Symptoms." *European Journal of Pediatrics* 171: 1549–57.

Asher, S.R., J.G. Parker, & D. Walker. 1996. "Distinguishing Friendship from Acceptance: Implications for Intervention and Assessment." In *The Company They Keep: Friendships in Childhood and Adolescence*, edited by W.M. Bukowski, A.F. Newcomb, & W.W. Hartup, 366–405. New York, NY: Cambridge University Press.

Atlas, R.S., & D.J. Pepler. 1998. "Observations of Bullying in the Classroom." *Journal of Educational Research* 92 (2): 86–99.

Auerbach, S. 2009. "Screening Out Cyberbullies: Remedies for Victims on the Internet Playground." *Cardozo Law Review* 30: 1641–75.

Barlińska, J., A. Szuster, & M. Winiewski. 2013. "Cyberbullying among Adolescent Bystanders: Role of the Communication Medium, Form of Violence, and Empathy." *Journal of Community & Applied Social Psychology* 23 (1): 37–51.

Bauman, S. 2009. "Cyberbullying in a Rural Intermediate School: An Exploratory Study." *Journal of Early Adolescence* 20 (10): 1–31.

Bauman, S. & A. Del Rio. 2006. "Preservice Teachers' Responses to Bullying Scenarios: Comparing Physical, Verbal, and Relational Bullying." *Journal of Educational Psychology* 98 (1): 219–31.

Beale, A.V., & K.R. Hall. 2007. "Cyberbullying: What School Administrators (and Parents) Can Do." *The Clearinghouse* 81 (1): 8–13.

Beaty, L.A., & E.B. Alexeyev. 2008. "The Problem of School Bullies: What the Research Tells Us." *Adolescence* 43 (169): 1–11.

Beran, T. 2008. "Stability of Harassment in Children: Analysis of the Canadian National Longitudinal Survey of Children and Youth Data." *The Journal of Psychology* 142 (2): 131–46.

Beran, T.N., G. Hughes, & J. Lupart. 2008. "A Model of Achievement and Bullying: Analyses of the Canadian National Longitudinal Survey of Children and Youth Data." *Educational Research* 50 (1): 25–39.

Beran, T., & Q. Li. 2005. "Cyber-harassment: A Study of a New Method for an Old Behavior." *Journal of Educational Computing Research* 32 (3): 265–77.

Beran, T.N., & J. Lupart. 2009. "The Relationship between School Achievement and Peer Harassment in Canadian Adolescents: The Importance of Mediating Factors." *School Psychology International* 30 (1): 75–91.

Beran, T.N., F. Mishna, R. Hetherington, & S. Shariff. Forthcoming. "Children's Experiences of Cyber-bullying: A Canadian National Study." *International Journal of Health Research.*

Beran, T.N., L. Tutty, & G. Steinrath. 2004. "An Evaluation of a Bullying Prevention Program for Elementary Schools." *Canadian Journal of School Psychology* 19 (1/2): 99–116.

Berndt, T. J., & S.G. Hoyle. 1985. "Stability and Change in Childhood and Adolescent Friendships." *Developmental Psychology* 21 (6): 1007–15.

Black, S., E. Washington, V. Trent, P. Harner, & E. Pollock. 2010. "Translating the Olweus Bullying Prevention Program into Real-World Practice." *Health Promotion Practice* 11 (5): 733–40.

Blais, J. 2008. *Chatting, Befriending, and Bullying: Adolescents' Internet Experiences and Associated Psychosocial Outcomes.* Unpublished PhD diss., Queen's University, Kingston, Ontario.

Blais, J., W.M. Craig, D.J. Pepler, & J. Connolly. 2008. "Adolescents Online: The Importance of Internet Activity Choices to Salient Relationships." *Journal of Youth and Adolescence* 37 (5): 49–58.

Blosnich, J., & R. Bossarte. 2011. "Low-level Violence in Schools: Is There an Association between School Safety Measures and Peer Victimization?" *Journal of School Health* 81 (2): 107–13.

Blumenfeld, W.J., & R.M. Cooper. 2010. "LGBT and Allied Youth Responses to Cyberbullying: Policy Implications." *International Journal of Critical Pedagogy* 3 (1): 114–33.

Bogard, M. 1999. "Strengthening Domestic Violence Theories: Intersections of Race, Class, Sexual Orientation, and Gender." *Journal of Marital and Family Therapy* 25 (3): 275–89.

Bonanno, R., & S. Hymel. 2013. "Cyber Bullying and Internalizing Difficulties: Above and Beyond the Impact of Traditional Forms of Bullying." *Journal of Youth and Adolescence* 42 (5): 685–97.

Boyd, D., & A. Marwick. 2011. "Bullying as True Drama." *The New York Times,* 22 September. Accessed 1 February 2014. www.nytimes.com/2011/09/23/opinion/why-cyberbullying-rhetoric-misses-the-mark.html.

Brendtro, L.K. 2001. "Worse than Sticks and Stones: Lessons from Research on Ridicule." *Reclaiming Children and Youth* 10 (1): 47–51.

Bronfenbrenner, U. 1979. *The Ecology of Human Development.* Cambridge, MA: Harvard University Press.

————. 1994. "Ecological Models of Human Development." In *International Encyclopedia of Education*, vol. 3, 2nd ed., 1643–47. Oxford: Elsevier.

Brown, K., M. Jackson, & W. Cassidy. 2006. "Cyber-bullying: Developing Policy to Direct Responses That Are Equitable and Effective in Addressing this Special Form of Bullying." *Canadian Journal of Educational Administration and Policy* 57. Accessed 20 April 2012. www.umanitoba.ca/publications/cjeap/articles/brown_jackson_cassidy.html.

Bruner, J.S. 1971. *The Relevance of Education.* New York: Norton.

Bumpus, M.F. & N.E. Werner. 2009. "Maternal Rule-Setting for Children's Internet Use." *Marriage and Family Review* 45 (6): 845–65.

Butler, D.A., S.M. Kift, M.A. Campbell, P. Slee, & B, Spears. 2011. "School Policy Responses to Cyber Bullying: An Australian Legal Perspective." *International Journal of Law and Education* 16 (2): 7–28.

Campbell, M.A. 2005. "Cyber Bullying: An Old Problem in a New Guise?" *Australian Journal of Guidance & Counselling* 15 (1): 68–76.

————. 2013. "How Research Findings Can Inform Legislation and School Policy on Cyber Bullying." In *Principles of Cyberbullying Research: Definition, Methods, and Measures*, edited by S. Bauman, J. Walker, & D. Cross, 261–73. New York & London: Routledge.

Campbell, M., B. Spears, P. Slee, D. Butler, & S. Kift. 2012. "Victims' Perceptions of Traditional and Cyberbullying, and the Psychosocial Correlates of Their Victimisation." *Emotional and Behavioural Difficulties* 17 (3/4): 389–401.

Canadian Council on Social Development. 2003. *Disability Information Sheet, No. 10, 11 and 12.* Accessed 24 November 2006. www.ccsd.ca/drip/research/.

————. 2006. *The Progress of Canada's Children and Youth 2006.* Ottawa: CCSD.

Cappadocia, M.C., J.A. Weiss, & D. Pepler. 2012. "Bullying Experiences among Children and Youth with Autism Spectrum Disorders." *Journal of Autism and Developmental Disorders* 42: 266–77.

Carter, B.B., & V.G. Spencer. 2006. "The Fear Factor: Bullying and Students with Disabilities." *International Journal of Special Education* 21: 11–20.

Cash, S.J., & J.A. Bridge. 2009. "Epidemiology of Youth Suicide and Suicidal Behavior." *Current Opinion in Pediatrics* 21 (5): 613–19.

Cassidy, W., M. Jackson, & K.N. Brown. 2009. "Sticks and Stones Can Break My Bones, But How Can Pixels Hurt Me? Students' Experiences with Cyber-bullying." *School Psychology International* 30 (4): 383–402.

Catanzaro, M.F. 2011. "Indirect Aggression, Bullying and Female Teen Victimization: A Literature Review." *Pastoral Care in Education* 29 (2): 83–101.

Champion, K., E. Vernberg, & K. Shipman. 2003. "Nonbullying Victims of Bullies: Aggression, Social Skills, and Friendship Characteristics." *Applied Developmental Psychology* 24: 535–51.

Chesir-Teran, D. 2003. "Conceptualizing and Assessing Heterosexism in High Schools: A Setting-Level Approach." *American Journal of Community Psychology* 31: 267–79.

Chiodo, D., D.A. Wolfe, C. Crooks, R. Hughes, & P. Jaffe. 2009. "Impact of Sexual Harassment Victimization by Peers on Subsequent Adolescent Victimization and Adjustment: A Longitudinal Study." *Journal of Adolescent Health* 45: 246–52.

Choi, S., & Y. Cho. 2012. "Influence of Psychological and Social Factors on Bystanders' Roles in School Bullying among Korean-American Students in the United States." *School Psychology International* 34 (1): 67–81.

Clarke, E.A., & M.S. Kiselica. 1997. "A Systemic Counseling Approach to the Problem of Bullying." *Elementary School Guidance & Counseling* 31 (4): 310–25.

Collier, A. 2012. "A 'Living Internet': Some Context for the Cyberbullying Discussion." In *Cyber Bullying Prevention and Response: Expert Perspectives*, edited by J.W. Patchin & S. Hinduja, 1–12. New York: Routledge.

Collins, P. 2000. *Black Feminist Thought: Knowledge, Consciousness, and the Politics of Empowerment*. New York: Routledge.

Cool, J. 2010. *Wage Gap between Women and Men*. Ottawa: Parliament of Canada.

Copeland, W.E., D. Wolke, A. Angold, & E.J. Costello. 2013. "Adult Psychiatric Outcomes of Bullying and Being Bullied by Peers in Childhood and Adolescence." *JAMA Psychiatry* 70 (4): 419–26.

Cowie, H., N. Hutson, O. Oztug, & C. Myers. 2008. "The Impact of Peer Support Schemes on Pupils' Perceptions of Bullying, Aggression and Safety at School." *Emotional and Behavioural Difficulties* 13 (1): 63–71.

Craig, K., D. Bell, & A. Leschied. 2011. "Pre-service Teachers' Knowledge and Attitudes Regarding School-Based Bullying." *Canadian Journal of Education* 34 (2): 21–33.

Craig, W.M. & Y. Harel. 2004. "Bullying, Physical Fighting and Victimization." In *Young People's Health in Context: International Report from the HBSC 2001/02 Survey*, edited by C. Currie, C. Roberts, A. Morgan, R. Smith, W. Settertobulte, O. Samdal, & V. Barnekow Rasmussen, 133–44. *WHO Policy Series: Health Policy for Children and Adolescents*, Issue 4. Copenhagen: WHO Regional Office for Europe.

Craig, W.M., Y. Harel-Fisch, H. Fogel-Grinvald, S. Dostaler, J. Hetland, B. Simons-Morton, et al. 2009. "A Cross-National Profile of Bullying and Victimization among Adolescents in 40 Countries." *International Journal of Public Health* 54 (suppl. 2): 216–24.

Craig, W., & D. Pepler. 2007. "Understanding Bullying: From Research to Practice." *Canadian Psychology/Psychologie Canadienne* 48 (2): 86–93.

Craig, W.M., D. Pepler, & R. Atlas. 2000. "Observations of Bullying in the Playground and in the Classroom." *School Psychology International* 21 (1): 22–36.

Craig, W., D. Pepler, & J. Blais. 2007. "Responding to Bullying: What Works?" *School Psychology International* 28 (4): 465–77.

Craig, W., D. Pepler, & J. Cummings. 2013. *Bullying Prevention: What Parents Need to Know*. Tucson, AZ: Quickfind Books.

Crick, N.R. 1996. "The Role of Overt Aggression, Relational Aggression, and Prosocial Behavior in the Prediction of Children's Future Social Adjustment." *Child Development* 67 (5): 2317–27.

Crick, N.R., & M.A. Bigbee. 1998. "Relational and Overt Forms of Peer Victimization: A Multi-informant Approach." *Journal of Consulting and Clinical Psychology* 66 (2): 337–47.

Crick, N.R., J.F. Casas, & H. Ku. 1999. "Relational and Physical Forms of Peer Victimization in Preschool." *Developmental Psychology* 35 (2): 376–85.

Crick, N.R., & J.K. Grotpeter. 1995. "Relational Aggression, Gender, and Social-Psychological Adjustment." *Child Development* 66: 710–22.

———. 1996. "Children's Treatment by Peers: Victims of Relational and Overt Aggression." *Development and Psychopathology* 8: 367–80.

Crick, N.R., J.K. Grotpeter, & M.A. Bigbee. 2002. "Relationally and Physically Aggressive Children's Intent Attributions and Feelings of Distress for Relational and Instrumental Peer Provocations." *Child Development* 73 (4): 1134–42.

Crick, N.R., & D.A. Nelson. 2002. "Relational and Physical Victimization within Friendships: Nobody Told Me There'd Be Friends Like These." *Journal of Abnormal Child Psychology* 30 (6): 599–607.

Cross, D., & J. Walker. 2013. "Using Research to Inform Cyberbullying Prevention and Intervention." In *Principles of Cyberbullying Research: Definition, Methods, and Measures*, edited by S. Bauman, J. Walker, & D. Cross, 274–92. New York & London: Routledge.

Cover, R. 2012. "Mediating Suicide: Print Journalism and the Categorization of Queer Youth Suicide Discourses." *Archives of Sexual Behavior* 41 (5): 1173–83.

Cullerton-Sen, C., & N.R. Crick. 2005. "Understanding the Effects of Physical and Relational Victimization: The Utility of Multiple Perspectives in Predicting Social-Emotional Adjustment." *School Psychology Review* 34 (2): 147–60.

Currie, D.H., D.M. Kelly, & S. Pomerantz. 2007. "The Power to Squash People: Understanding Girls' Relational Aggression." *British Journal of Sociology of Education* 28 (1): 23–37.

Daley, A., S. Solomon, P.A. Newman, & F. Mishna. 2008. "Traversing the Margins: Intersectionalities in the Bullying of Lesbian, Gay, Bisexual, and Transgender Youth." *Journal of Gay and Lesbian Social Services* 19 (3/4): 9–29.

Davis, S., P. Howell, & F. Cooke. 2002. "Sociodynamic Relationships between Children Who Stutter and Their Non-stuttering Classmates." *Journal of Child Psychology and Psychiatry* 43 (7): 939–47.

Dawkins, H.L. 1996. "Bullying, Physical Disability and the Pediatric Patient." *Developmental Medicine and Child Neurology* 38 (7): 603–12.

Dehue, F., C. Bolman, & T. Vollink. 2008. "Cyberbullying: Youngsters' Experiences and Parental Perception." *Cyberpsychology & Behavior* 11 (2): 217–25.

deLara, E.W. 2012. "Why Adolescents Don't Disclose Incidents of Bullying and Harassment." *Journal of School Violence* 11: 288–305.

Dickerson, D. 2009. "What is Cyberbullying?" *NASPA Leadership Exchange* 29 (March). Accessed 1 February 2014. http://ssrn.com/abstract=1375150.

Dooley, J.J., J. Pyzalski, & D. Cross. 2009. "Cyberbullying versus Face-to-Face Bullying: A Theoretical and Conceptual Review." *Journal of Psychology* 217 (4): 182–88.

Dowden, C., & S. Brennan. 2012. *Police-Reported Hate Crime in Canada, 2010*. Juristat Article, Catalogue no.85-002-X. Ottawa, ON: Statistics Canada.

Drolet, M., M. Paquin, & M. Soutyrine. 2006. "Building Collaboration between School and Parents: Issues for School Social Workers and Parents Whose Young Children Exhibit Violent Behavior at School." *European Journal of Social Work* 9 (2): 201–22.

Due, P., B.E. Holstein, J. Lynch, F. Diderichsen, S.N. Gabhain, P. Scheidt, et al. 2005. "Bullying and Symptoms among School-Aged Children: International Comparative Cross Sectional Study in 28 Countries." *European Journal of Public Health* 15 (2): 128–32.

Duncan, N. 1999. *Sexual Bullying: Gender Conflict and Pupil Culture in Secondary Schools*. New York: Routledge.

Duncan, R.D. 1999. Peer and Sibling Aggression: An Investigation of Intra- and Extra-familial Bullying. *Journal of Interpersonal Violence* 14 (8): 871–86.

Dupper, D.R. 2003. *School Social Work: Skills and Interventions for Effective Practice*. Hoboken, NJ: Wiley.

Dupper, D., & N. Meyer-Adams. 2002. "Low-Level Violence—A Neglected Aspect of School Culture." *Urban Education* 37 (3): 350–64.

Elinoff, M.J., S.M. Chafouleas, & K.A. Sassu. 2004. "Bullying: Considerations for Defining and Intervening in School Settings." *Psychology in the Schools* 41 (8): 887–97.

Elwell, L., S. Grogan, & N. Coulson. 2010. "Adolescents Living with Cancer: The Role of Computer-Mediated Support Groups." *Journal of Health Psychology* 16 (2): 236–48.

Elze, D.E. 2003. "Gay, Lesbian, and Bisexual Youths' Perceptions of their High School Environments and Comfort Zone." *Children and Schools* 25 (4): 225–39.

Engel, G.L. 1977. "The Need of a New Medical Model: A Challenge for Biomedicine." *Science* 196: 129–36.

Englander, E.K., & C. Lawson. 2007. "New Approaches to Preventing Peer Abuse among Children." In *Play Therapy with Children in Crisis*, 3rd ed., edited by N.B. Webb, 37–56. New York, NY: The Guilford Press.

Ensor, R., A. Marks, L. Jacobs, & C. Hughes. 2010. "Trajectories of Antisocial Behaviour towards Siblings Predict Antisocial Behaviour towards Peers." *The Journal of Child Psychology and Psychiatry* 51 (11): 1208–16.

Espelage, D.L., & S.M. Swearer. 2003. "Research on School Bullying and Victimization: What Have We Learned and Where Do We Go from Here?" *School Psychology Review* 32 (3): 365–74.

Farrington, D.P., A.C. Baldry, B. Kyvsgaard, & M.M. Ttofi. 2008. "Systematic Review Protocol: Effectiveness of Programs to Prevent School Bullying." Oslo: Nordic Campbell Centre. Accessed 5 November 2008. www.campbellcollaboration.org/lib/download/382/.

Felix, E., & S. McMahon. 2006. "Gender and Multiple Forms of Peer Victimization: How Do They Influence Adolescent Psychosocial Adjustment." *Violence and Victims* 21 (6): 707–24.

Ferguson, C.J., C. San Miguel, J.C. Kilburn, Jr., & P. Sanchez. 2007. "The Effectiveness of School-Based Anti-bullying Programs: A Meta-analytic Review." *Criminal Justice Review* 32 (4): 401–14.

Fineran, S., & R.M. Bolen. 2006. "Risk Factors for Peer Sexual Harassment in Schools." *Journal of Interpersonal Violence* 21 (9): 1169–90.

Finkelhor, D. 1995. "The Victimization of Children: A Developmental Perspective." *American Journal of Orthopsychiatry* 65 (2): 177–93.

Finkelhor, D., H.A. Turner, & S. Hamby. 2012. "Let's Prevent Peer Victimization, Not Just Bullying." *Child Abuse & Neglect* 36: 271–74.

Gasser, U., C.M. Maclay, & J.G. Palfrey. 2010. "Working towards a Deeper Understanding of Digital Safety for Children and Young People in Developing Nations." *Harvard Public Law Working Paper* (10–36). Accessed 1 February 2014. http://ssrn.com/abstract=1628276.

Goldstein, S.E., & M.S. Tisak. 2004. "Adolescents' Outcome Expectancies about Relational Aggression within Acquaintanceships, Friendships, and Dating Relationships." *Journal of Adolescence* 27 (3): 283–302.

Goldweber, A., T.E. Waasdorp, & C.P. Bradshaw. 2013. "Examining Associations between Race, Urbanicity, and Patterns of Bullying Involvement." *Journal of Youth and Adolescence* 42 (2): 206–19.

Goodno, N.H. 2007. "Cyberstalking, a New Crime: Evaluating the Effectiveness of Current State and Federal Laws." *Missouri Law Review* 72: 125–97.

Graham, S. 2006. "Peer Victimization in School: Exploring the Ethnic Context." *Current Directions in Psychological Science* 15 (6): 317–21.

Greene, M.B. 2006. "Bullying in Schools: A Plea for Measure of Human Rights." *Journal of Social Issues* 62 (1): 63–79.

Griffith, B., & G. Labercane. 1995. "High School Students' Attitudes towards Racism in Canada: A Report on a 1993 Cross-cultural Study." In *Multicultural Education: The State of the Art, Report #2*, edited by K. A. McLeod, 144–51. Winnipeg, MB: Canadian Association of Second Language Teachers. Accessed 18 April 2011. www.lang canada.ca/pdf/high_school.pdf.

Guerin, S., & E. Hennessy. 2002. "Pupils' Definitions of Bullying." *European Journal of Psychology of Education* 17 (3): 249–62.

Guerra, N.G., A.A. Williamson, & S. Sadek. 2012. "Youth Perspectives on Bullying in Adolescence." *The Prevention Researcher* 19: 14–16.

Harel-Fisch, Y., S.D. Walsh, H. Fogel-Grinvald, G. Amitai, W. Pickett, M. Molcho, et al. 2011. "Negative School Perceptions and Involvement in School Bullying: A Universal Relationship across 40 Countries." *Journal of Adolescence* 34: 639–52.

Hawker, D.S.J., & M.J. Boulton. 2000. "Twenty Years' Research on Peer Victimization and Psychosocial Maladjustment: A Meta-analytic Review of Cross-sectional Studies." *Journal of Child Psychology and Psychiatry* 41 (4): 441–55.

Hawkins, D.L., & W.M. Craig. 2001. "Naturalistic Observations of Peer Interventions in Bullying." *Social Development* 10 (4): 512–27.

Haynie, D.L., T. Nansel, P. Eitel, A.D. Crump, K. Saylor, K. Yu, et al. 2001. "Bullies, Victims, and Bully/Victims: Distinct Groups of At-Risk Youth." *Journal of Early Adolescence* 21 (1): 29–49.

Hazler, R.J., D.L. Miller, J.V. Carney, & S. Green. 2001. "Adult Recognition of School Bullying Situations." *Educational Research* 43 (2): 133–46.

Heidlage, B. 2009. "A Relational Approach to Schools' Regulation of Youth Online Speech." *New York University Law Review* 84: 572–608.

Herrenkohl, T.I., B.J. McMorris, R.F. Catalano, R.D. Abbott, S.A. Hemphill, & J.W. Toumbourou. 2007. "Risk Factors for Violence and Relational Aggression in Adolescence." *Journal of Interpersonal Violence* 22 (4): 386–405.

Hinduja, S., & J.W. Patchin. 2008. "Cyberbullying: An Exploratory Analysis of Factors Related to Offending and Victimization." *Deviant Behaviour* 29 (2): 129–56.

———. 2009. *Bullying Beyond the Schoolyard: Preventing and Responding to Cyberbullying.* Thousand Oaks, CA: Sage Publications.

———. 2010. "Bullying, Cyberbullying, and Suicide." *Archives of Suicide Research* 14: 206–21.

Hodges, E.V.E., M. Boivin, F. Vitaro, & W.M. Bukowski. 1999. "The Power of Friendship: Protection against an Escalating Cycle of Peer Victimization." *Developmental Psychology* 35 (1): 94–101.

Hugh-Jones, S., & P.K. Smith. 1999. "Self-Reports of Short- and Long-Term Effects of Bullying on Children Who Stammer." *British Journal of Educational Psychology* 69 (2): 141–58.

Hunter, S.C., J.M.E. Boyle, & D. Warden. 2004. "Help Seeking amongst Child and Adolescent Victims of Peer-Aggression and Bullying: The Influence of School-Stage, Gender, Victimization, Appraisal, and Emotion." *British Journal of Educational Psychology* 74 (3): 375–90.

Hymel, S., N.R. Rocke-Henderson, & R.A. Bonanno. 2005. "Moral Disengagement: A Framework for Understanding Bullying among Adolescents." *Journal of Social Sciences* 8: 1–11.

Jackson, L.A., A. von Eye, F.A. Biocca, G. Barbatsis, Y. Zhao, & H.E. Fitzgerald. 2006. "Does Home Internet Use Influence the Academic Performance of Low-Income Children?" *Developmental Psychology* 42 (3): 429–35.

Jaffer, The Honourable M.S.B., & The Honourable, P. Brazeau. 2012. "Cyberbullying Hurts: Respect for Rights in the Digital Age." Standing Senate Committee on Human Rights. Ottawa, ON: Government of Canada.

Janoff, D.V. 2005. *Pink Blood: Homophobic Violence in Canada.* Toronto, ON: University of Toronto Press.

Johnson, G.M. 2010. "Internet Use and Child Development: The Techno-microsystem." *Australian Journal of Educational & Developmental Psychology* 10: 32–43.

Johnson, G. M., & P. Puplampu. 2008. "A Conceptual Framework for Understanding the Effect of the Internet on Child Development: The Ecological Techno-subsystem." *Canadian Journal of Learning and Technology* 34: 19–28.

Juvonen, J., & A. Galvan. 2008. "Peer Influence in Involuntary Social Groups: Lessons from Research on Bullying." In *Understanding Peer Influence in Children and Adolescents*, edited by M.J. Prinstein & K.A. Dodge, 225–44. New York, NY: Guilford Press.

Juvonen, J., & E.G. Gross. 2008. "Extending the School Ground? Bullying Experiences in Cyberspace?" *Journal of School Health* 78: 496–505.

Juvonen, J., A. Nishina, & S. Graham. 2006. "Ethnic Diversity and Perceptions of Safety in Urban Middle Schools." *Psychological Science* 17: 393–400.

Kärnä, A., M. Voeten, T.D. Little, E. Poskiparta, A. Kaljonen, & C. Salmivalli. 2011. "A Large-Scale Evaluation of the KiVa Antibullying Program: Grades 4–6." *Child Development* 82 (1): 311–30.

Khoury-Kassabri, M. 2009. "The Relationship between Staff Maltreatment of Students and Students' Violent Behavior." *Child Abuse & Neglect* 33: 914–23.

Kimmel, M.S., & M. Mahler. 2003. "Adolescent Masculinity, Homophobia and Violence." *American Behavioural Scientist* 46 (10): 1439–58.

Klomek, A.B., A. Sourander, & M. Gould. 2010. "The Association of Suicide and Bullying in Childhood to Young Adulthood: A Review of Cross-sectional and Longitudinal Research Findings." *Canadian Journal of Psychiatry* 55 (5): 282–89.

Konishi, C., S. Hymel, B.D. Zumbo, & Z. Li. 2010. "Do School Bullying and Student-Teacher Relationships Matter for Academic Achievement? A Multilevel Analysis." *Canadian Journal of School Psychology* 25 (1): 19–39.

Kosciw, J., M. Bartkiewicz, & E.A. Greytak. 2012. "Promising Strategies for Prevention of the Bullying of Lesbian, Gay, Bisexual, and Transgender Youth." *The Prevention Researcher* 19 (3): 10–13.

Kowalchuk, K., & S. Crompton. 2009. "Social Participation of Children with Disabilities." *Canadian Social Trends, Living with a Disability* series. Catalogue no. 11-008-X. Ottawa: Statistics Canada.

Kowalski, R.M., G.W. Giumetti, A.N. Schroeder, & M.R. Lattanner. 2014. "Bullying in the Digital Age: A Critical Review and Meta-analysis of Cyberbullying Research among Youth." *Psychological Bulletin*. Accessed 4 April 2014. doi: 10.1037/a0035618.

Kowalski, R.M., & S.P. Limber. 2007. "Electronic Bullying among Middle School Students." *Journal of Adolescent Health* 41: S22–S30.

Kowalski, R., S. Limber, & P.W. Agatston. 2008. *Cyber Bullying*. Malden, MA: Blackwell Publishing.

Kowalski, R., C. Morgan, & S. Limber. 2012. "Traditional Bullying as a Potential Warning Sign of Cyberbullying." *School Psychology International* 33 (5): 505–19.

Kumpulainen, K., E. Räsänen, & K. Puura. 2001. "Psychiatric Disorders and the Use of Mental Health Services among Children Involved in Bullying." *Aggressive Behavior* 27 (2): 102–10.

Land, D. 2003. "Teasing Apart Secondary Students' Conceptualizations of Peer Teasing, Bullying and Sexual Harassment." *School Psychology International* 24 (2): 147–65.

Larochette, A.C., A.N. Murphy, & W. Craig. 2010. "Racial Bullying and Victimization in Canadian School-Aged Children: Individual and School Level Effects." *School Psychology International* 31 (4): 389–408.

Law, D.M., J.D. Shapka, S. Hymel, B.F. Olson, & T. Waterhouse. 2012. "The Changing Face of Bullying: An Empirical Comparison between Traditional and Internet Bullying and Victimization." *Computers in Human Behavior* 28: 226–32.

Lee, C. 2006. "Exploring Teachers' Definitions of Bullying." *Emotional & Behavioural Difficulties* 11 (1): 61–75.

Lemstra, M., M. Rogers, L. Redgate, M. Garner, & J. Moraros. 2011. "Prevalence, Risk Indicators and Outcomes of Bullying among On-Reserve First Nations Youth." *Canadian Journal of Public Health* 102 (6): 462–66.

Lewit, E.M., & L.S. Baker. 1996. "Children as Victims of Violence." *The Future of Children* 6 (3): 147–56.

Li, Q. 2007. "Bullying in the New Playground: Research into Cyberbullying and Cyber Victimisation." *Australasian Journal of Educational Technology* 23 (4): 435–54.

Lindsay, S., & A.C. McPherson. 2012. "Experiences of Social Exclusion and Bullying at School among Children with Cerebral Palsy." *Disability and Rehabilitation* 34 (2): 101–9.

Little, L. 2002. "Middle-Class Mothers' Perceptions of Peer and Sibling Victimization among Children with Asperger's Syndrome and Nonverbal Learning Disorders." *Issues in Comprehensive Pediatric Nursing* 25: 43–57.

Litwiller, B., & A. Brausch. 2013. "Cyber Bullying and Physical Bullying in Adolescent Suicide: The Role of Violent Behavior and Substance Use." *Journal of Youth and Adolescence* 42 (5): 675–84.

Livingstone, S. 2007. "Strategies of Parental Regulation in the Media-Rich Home." *Computers in Human Behavior* 23: 920–41.

Livingstone, S., & M. Bober. 2004. *UK Children Go Online: Surveying the Experiences of Young People and Their Parents.* London: LSE Research Online. Retrieved 20 April 2011. http://eprints.lse.ac.uk/archive/0000395.

Livingstone, S, & L. Haddon. 2009. *EU Kids Online: Final Report.* London: LSE, EU Kids Online.

Macháčková, H., L. Dedkova, A. Sevcikova, & A. Cerna. 2013. "Bystanders' Support of Cyberbullied Schoolmates." *Journal of Community & Applied Social Psychology* 23 (1): 25–36.

Mallon, G. 2001. "Sticks and Stones Can Break Your Bones: Verbal Harassment and Physical Violence in the Lives of Gay and Lesbian Youth in Child Welfare Settings." *Journal of Gay and Lesbian Social Services* 13 (1/2): 63–81.

Marini, Z.A., & A.V. Dane. 2008. "Matching Interventions to Bullying Subtypes: Ensuring Programs Fit the Multifaceted Needs of Children Involved in Bullying." In *An International Perspective on Understanding and Addressing Bullying,* edited by D. Pepler & W. Craig, 97–126. PREVNet Series vol. 1. Bloomington, IN: Authorhouse.

Martin, J. 2010. "To Be Seen… Not Heard: Understanding the Harms Done to Children Made the Subject of Child Sexual Abuse Images on the Internet." Unpublished manuscript. University of Toronto, Toronto, Ontario.

———. (2013). Out of Focus: Exploring Practitioners' Understanding of Child Sexual Abuse Images on the Internet. Unpublished PhD diss., University of Toronto, Toronto, Ontario.

Martin, J., & R. Alaggia. 2013. "Sexual Abuse Images in Cyberspace: Expanding the Ecology of the Child." *Journal of Child Sexual Abuse* 22 (4): 398–415.

Martin J., & C. Stuart. 2011. "Working with Cyberspace in the Life-Space." *Relational Child & Youth Care Practice* 24 (1/2): 55–66.

Martinelli, V., N. Brondino, R. Rossi, R. Panigati, M. Magnani, L. Cappucciati, et al. 2011. "Bullying Behaviours among Students in Pavia, Italy: Prevalence and Association with Stress and Cannabis Use." *Epidemiology and Psychiatric Sciences* 20: 339–43.

McCaskill, D. 2012. "Discrimination and Public Perceptions of Aboriginal People in Canadian Cities." Ottawa, ON: Urban Aboriginal Knowledge Network. Accessed 3 November 2013. http://uakn.org/wp-content/uploads/2013/01/Discrimination-and-Public-Perceptions-of-Aboriginal-People-in-Canadian-Cities-McCaskill.pdf.

McKenney, K.S., D. Pepler, W. Craig, & J. Connolly. 2006. "Peer Victimization and Psychosocial Adjustment: The Experiences of Canadian Immigrant Youth." *Journal of Research in Educational Psychology* 9 (4): 239–64.

McMaster, L.E., J. Connolly, D. Pepler, & W.M. Craig. 2002. "Peer to Peer Sexual Harassment in Early Adolescence: A Developmental Perspective." *Development and Psychopathology* 14 (1): 91–105.

Menesini, E., M. Camodeca, & A. Nocentini. 2010. "Bullying among Siblings: The Role of Personality and Relational Variables." *British Journal of Developmental Psychology* 28: 921–39.

Menesini, E., E. Codecasa, B. Benelli, & H. Cowie. 2003. "Enhancing Children's Responsibility to Take Action against Bullying: Evaluation of a Befriending Intervention in Italian Middle Schools." *Aggressive Behavior* 29 (1): 1–14.

Mesch, G.S. 2006. "Family Relations and the Internet: Exploring a Family Boundaries Approach." *Journal of Family Communication* 6 (2): 119–38.

Meyer, I. 2003. "Prejudice, Social Stress, and Mental Health in Lesbian, Gay, and Bisexual Populations: Conceptual Issues and Research Evidence." *Psychological Bulletin* 129 (5): 674–97.

Milan, A., M. Vezina, & C. Wells. 2007. *Family Portrait: Continuity and Change in Canadian Families and Households in 2006, 2006 Census*. Ottawa: Statics Canada.

Mishna, F. 2004. "A Qualitative Study of Bullying from Multiple Perspectives." *Children & Schools* 26 (4): 234–47.

———. 2012. *Bullying: A Guide to Research, Intervention, and Prevention*. New York: Oxford University Press.

Mishna, F., & R. Alaggia. 2005. "Weighing the Risks: A Child's Decision to Disclose Peer Victimization." *Children & Schools* 27 (4): 217–26.

Mishna, F., C. Cook, T. Gadalla, J. Daciuk, & S. Solomon. 2010. "Cyber Bullying Behaviors among Middle and High School Students." *American Journal of Orthopsychiatry* 80 (3): 362–74.

Mishna, F., M. Khoury-Kassabri, T. Gadalla, & J. Daciuk. 2012. "Risk Factors for Involvement in Cyber Bullying: Victims, Bullies and Bully-Victims." *Children and Youth Services Review* 34: 63–70.

Mishna, F., A. McLuckie, & M. Saini. 2009. "Real World Dangers in an Online Reality: A Qualitative Study Examining Online Relationships and Cyber Abuse." *Social Work Research* 33 (2): 107–18.

Mishna, F., P.A. Newman, A. Daley, & S. Solomon. 2009. "Bullying of Lesbian and Gay Youth: A Qualitative Investigation." *British Journal of Social Work* 39 (8): 1598–614.

Mishna, F., D. Pepler, C. Cook, W. Craig, & J. Wiener. 2010. "The Ongoing Problem of Bullying in Canada: A Ten-Year Perspective." *Canadian Social Work* 12 (2): 43–59.

Mishna, F., D. Pepler, & J. Wiener. 2006. "Factors Associated with Perceptions and Responses to Bullying Situations by Children, Parents, Teachers and Principals." *Victims and Offenders* 1 (3): 255–88.

Mishna, F., M. Saini, & S. Solomon. 2009. "Ongoing and Online: Children and Youth's Perceptions of Cyber Bullying." *Children and Youth Services Review* 31: 1222–28.

Mishna, F., I. Scarcello, D. Pepler, & J. Wiener. 2005. "Teachers' Understanding of Bullying." *Canadian Journal of Education* 28 (4): 718–38.

Mishna, F., J. Wiener, & D. Pepler. 2008. "Some of My Best Friends—Experiences of Bullying within Friendships." *School Psychology International* 29 (5): 549–73.

Mitchell, K.J., D. Finkelhor, & J. Wolak. 2007. "Online Requests for Sexual Pictures from Youth: Risk Factors and Incident Characteristics." *Journal of Adolescent Health* 41: 196–203.

Mitchell, K. J., M. Ybarra, & D. Finkelhor. 2007. "The Relative Importance of Online Victimization in Understanding Depression, Delinquency, and Substance Use." *Child Maltreatment* 12 (4): 314–24.

Modecki, K.L., B.L. Barber, & L. Vernon. 2013. "Mapping Developmental Precursors of Cyber-aggression: Trajectories of Risk Predict Perpetration and Victimization." *Journal of Youth and Adolescence* 42: 651–61.

Molcho, M., W. Craig, P. Due, W. Pickett, Y. Harel-Fisch, M. Overpeck, et al. 2009. "Cross-national Time Trends in Bullying Behaviour 1994–2006: Findings from Europe and North America." *International Journal of Public Health* 54: S225–S234.

Monks, C.P., & P.K. Smith. 2006. "Definitions of Bullying: Age Differences in Understanding of the Term, and the Role of Experience." *British Journal of Developmental Psychology* 24 (4): 801–21.

Murdock, T.B., & M.B. Bolch. 2005. "Risk and Protective Factors for Poor School Adjustment in Lesbian, Gay, and Bisexual (LGB) High School Youth: Variable and Person-Centered Analyses." *Psychology in the Schools* 42: 159–72.

Nangle, D.W., C.A. Erdley, J.E. Newman, C.A. Mason, & E.M. Carpenter. 2003. "Popularity, Friendship Quantity, and Friendship Quality: Interactive Influences on Children's Loneliness and Depression." *Journal of Clinical Child and Adolescent Psychology* 32 (4): 546–55.

Nansel, T.R., M. Overpeck, R.S. Pilla, W.J. Ruan, B. Simons-Morton, & P. Scheidt. 2001. "Bullying Behaviors among US Youth: Prevalence and Association with Psychosocial Adjustment." *JAMA* 285 (16): 2094–100.

Newcomb, A.F., & C.L. Bagwell. 1995. "Children's Friendship Relations: A Meta-analytic Review." *Psychological Bulletin* 117 (2): 306–47.

Ng, K. 2012. "Digital Dilemmas: Responding to Cyberbullying in Nova Scotia." *Education Law Journal* 22 (1): 63–91.

Norwich, B., & N. Kelly. 2004. "Pupils' Views on Inclusion: Moderate Learning Difficulties and Bullying in Mainstream and Special Schools." *British Educational Research Journal* 30 (1): 43–65.

O'Brien, C. 1994. "The Social Organization of the Treatment of Lesbian, Gay and Bisexual Youth in Group Homes and Youth Shelters." *Canadian Review of Social Policy* 34 (2): 37–57.

O'Connell, P., D. Pepler, & W. Craig. 1999. "Peer Involvement in Bullying: Insights and Challenges for Intervention." *Journal of Adolescence* 22 (4): 437–52.

Oliver, C., & M. Candappa. 2007. "Bullying and the Politics of 'Telling.'" *Oxford Review of Education* 33 (1): 71–86.

Olweus, D. 1984. "Aggressors and Their Victims: Bullying at School." In *Disruptive Behavior in Schools*, edited by N. Frude & H. Gault, 57–76. New York: John Wiley & Sons Ltd.

———. 1988. "Bullying in the Schools: How Educators Can Help." *The Education Digest* 53 (7): 30–34.

————. 1989. *Questionnaire for Students* (Junior and Senior versions). Unpublished manuscript.

————. 1991. "Bully/Victim Problems among School Children: Basic Facts and Effects of a School Based Intervention Program." In *The Development and Treatment of Childhood Aggression*, edited by D. Pepler & K. Rubin, 411–48. Hillsdale, NJ: Lawrence Erlbaum Associates.

————. 1992. "Bullying among School Children: Intervention and Prevention." In *Aggression and Violence throughout the Life Span*, edited by R.D. Peters, R.J. McMahon, & V.L. Quinsey, 100–25. London: Sage Publications.

————. 1993. *Bullying at School: What We Know and What We Can Do*. Oxford: Blackwell Publishers.

————. 1994. "Annotation: Bullying at School: Basic Facts and Effects of a School Based Intervention Program." *Journal of Child Psychology and Psychiatry and Allied Disciplines* 35 (7): 1171–90.

————. 1997. "Bully/Victim Problems in School: Facts and Interventions." *European Journal of Psychology of Education* 12 (4): 495–510.

————. 2004. "The Olweus Bullying Prevention Programme: Design and Implementation Issues and a New National Initiative in Norway." In *Bullying in Schools: How Successful Can Interventions Be?*, edited by P.K. Smith, D. Pepler, & K. Rigby, 13–36. Cambridge: Cambridge University Press.

————. 2013. "School Bullying: Development and Some Important Challenges." *Annual Review of Clinical Psychology* 9: 751–80.

Olweus, D., & S. Limber. 2010a. "Bullying in School: Evaluation and Dissemination of the Olweus Bullying Prevention Program." *American Journal of Orthopsychiatry* 80 (1): 124–34.

————. 2010b. "A Misunderstanding of 'Whole-School' Programs." St. Paul, MN: Minnesota Elementary School Principals' Association. Accessed 11 March 2014. www. mespa.net/A_Misunderstanding_of_Whole-School_Programs.html.

Olweus, D., S. Limber, & S. Mihalic. 2000. *Bullying Prevention Program* (Blueprints for Violence Prevention No. BP-009). Boulder, CO: Institute of Behavioral Science, Center for the Study and Prevention of Violence.

Owens, L., R. Shute, & P. Slee. 2000. "'Guess What I Just Heard!': Indirect Aggression among Teenage Girls in Australia." *Aggressive Behavior* 26: 67–83.

Patchin, J.W., & S. Hinduja. 2006. "Bullies Move Beyond the Schoolyard: A Preliminary Look at Cyberbullying." *Youth Violence and Juvenile Justice* 4 (2): 148–69.

————. 2010. "Cyberbullying and Self-Esteem." *Journal of School Health* 80 (12): 614–21.

————. 2012. "Cyberbullying: An Update and Synthesis of the Research." In *Cyber Bullying Prevention and Response: Expert Perspectives*, 13–35. New York: Routledge.

Pellegrini, A.D., & C. Roseth. 2006. "Relational Aggression and Relationships in Preschoolers: A Discussion of Methods, Gender Differences, and Function." *Journal of Applied Developmental Psychology* 27 (3): 269–76.

Pepler, D.J. 2006. "Bullying Interventions: A Binocular Perspective." *Journal of the Canadian Academy of Child and Adolescent Psychiatry* 15 (1): 16–20.

Pepler, D.J., J. Connolly, & W.M. Craig. 1993. *Safe School Questionnaire*. Unpublished manuscript.

————. 1999. *Bullying and Harassment: Experiences of Minority and Immigrant Youth*. CERIS report. Accessed 29 October 2013. http://ceris.metropolis.net/Virtual%20 Library/education/pepler1/pepler1.html.

Pepler, D.J., & W. Craig. 2011. "Promoting Relationships and Eliminating Violence in Canada." *International Journal of Behavioral Development* 35 (5): 389–97.

Pepler, D.J., W.M. Craig, P. O'Connell, R. Atlas, & A. Charach. 2004. "Making a Difference in Bullying: Evaluation of a Systemic School-Based Programme in Canada." In *Bullying in Schools: How Successful Can Interventions Be?*, edited by P.K. Smith, D. Pepler, & K. Rigby, 125–39. New York, NY: Cambridge University Press.

Pepler, D.J., W.M. Craig, S. Ziegler, & A. Charach. 1994. "An Evaluation of an Anti-bullying Intervention in Toronto Schools." *Canadian Journal of Community Mental Health* 13 (2): 95–110.

Pepler, D., D. Jiang, W. Craig, & J. Connolly. 2008. "Developmental Trajectories of Bullying and Associated Dactors." *Child Development* 79 (2): 325–38.

Pepler, D., P.K. Smith, & K. Rigby. 2004. "Looking Back and Looking Forward: Implications for Making Interventions Work Effectively." In *Bullying in Schools: How Successful Can Interventions Be?*, edited by P.K. Smith, D. Pepler, & K. Rigby, 307–24. New York, NY: Cambridge University Press.

Pilkington, J., & A. D'Augelli. 1995. "Victimization of Lesbian, Gay, and Bisexual Youth in Community Settings." *Journal of Community Psychology* 23 (1): 34–56.

Polanin, J.R., D.L. Espelage, & T.D. Pigott. 2012. "A Meta-analysis of School-Based Bullying Prevention Programs' Effects on Bystander Intervention Behavior." *School Psychology Review* 41 (1): 47–65.

Pornari, C.D., & J. Wood. 2010. "Peer and Cyber Aggression in Secondary School Students: The Role of Moral Disengagement, Hostile Attribution Bias, and Outcome Expectancies." *Aggressive Behavior* 36: 81–94.

Poteat, V.P., & D.L. Espelage. 2005. "Exploring the Relation between Bullying and Homophobic Verbal Content: The Homophobic Content Agent Target (HCAT) Scale." *Violence and Victims* 20 (5): 513–28.

———. 2007. "Predicting Psychosocial Consequences of Homophobic Victimization in Middle School Students." *Journal of Early Adolescence* 27 (2): 175–91.

Prensky, M. 2001. "Digital Natives, Digital Immigrants." *On the Horizon* 9 (5): 1–6.

PREVNet. 2014. "Why Should I Use PREVNet's BEST in My School?" Kingston, ON: PREVNet. Accessed 4 April 2014. www.prevnet.ca/resources/assessment-tool/about/why-should-i-use-prevnets-best-in-my-school.

Prinstein, M.J., & A.H.N. Cillessen. 2003. "Forms and Functions of Adolescent Peer Aggression Associated with High Levels of Peer Status." *Merrill-Palmer Quarterly* 49 (3): 310–42.

Rahimi, R., & D. Liston. 2011. "Race, Class, and Emerging Sexuality: Teacher Perceptions and Sexual Harassment in Schools." *Gender and Education* 23 (7). Accessed 15 November 2013. doi: 10.1080/09540253.2010.536143.

Ramya, S.G., & M.L. Kulkarni. 2011. "Bullying among School Children: Prevalence and Association with Common Symptoms in Childhood." *Indian Journal of Pediatrics* 78: 307–10.

Raskauskas, J., & A.D. Stoltz. 2007. "Involvement in Traditional and Electronic Bullying among Adolescents." *Developmental Psychology* 43 (3): 564–75.

Rideout, V.J., U.G. Foehr, & D.F. Roberts. 2010. *Generation M2. Media in the Lives of 8- to 18-Year-Olds.* Washington, DC: Henry J. Kaiser Foundation. www.kff.org.

Rigby, K. 2000. "Effects of Peer Victimization in Schools and Perceived Social Support on Adolescent Well-Being." *Journal of Adolescence* 23 (1): 57–68.

———. 2002. *New Perspectives on Bullying.* Philadelphia: Kinglsey.

————. 2003. "Consequences of Bullying in Schools." *Canadian Journal of Psychiatry* 48 (9): 583–90.

Robin, L., N.D. Brener, S.F. Donahue, T. Hack, K. Hale, & C. Goodenow. 2002. "Associations between Health Risk Behaviours and Opposite, Same, and Both-Sex Sexual Partners in Representative Samples of Vermont and Massachusetts High School Students." *Archives of Pediatrics and Adolescent Medicine* 156 (4): 349–55.

Rodkin, P.C., & K. Fischer. 2003. "Sexual Harassment and the Cultures of Childhood. Developmental, Domestic Violence, and Legal Perspectives." *Journal of Applied School Psychology* 19 (12): 177–96.

Roland, E. 2002. "Aggression, Depression, and Bullying Others." *Aggressive Behavior* 28: 198–206.

Roots of Empathy. 2009. *Report on Research 2009*. Accessed 3 March 2014. www.roots ofempathy.org/documents/content/ROE_Report_Research_E_2009.pdf.

Ruedy, M. 2008. "Repercussions of a MySpace Teen Suicide: Should Anti-cyberbullying Laws be Created?" *North Carolina Journal of Law and Technology* 9 (2): 323–46.

Russell, S.T., K.O. Sinclair, V.P. Poteat, & B.W. Koenig. 2012. "Adolescent Health and Harassment Based on Discriminatory Bias." *American Journal of Public Health* 102 (3): 493–95.

Ryan, C., & I. Rivers. 2003. "Lesbian, Gay, Bisexual and Transgender Youth: Victimization and its Correlates in the USA and UK." *Culture, Health and Sexuality* 5 (2): 103–19.

Saewyc, E.M. 2008. "Research on Adolescent Sexual Orientation: Development, Health Disparities, Stigma, and Resilience." *Journal of Research on Adolescence* 21 (1): 256–72.

Saewyc, E., C. Poon, N. Wang, Y. Homma, A. Smith, & the McCreary Centre Society. 2007. *Not Yet Equal: The Health of Lesbian, Gay, and Bisexual Youth in BC*. Vancouver, BC: McCreary Centre Society.

Sainio, M., R. Veenstra, G. Huitsing, & C. Salmivalli. 2011. "Victims and their Defenders: A Dyadic Approach." *International Journal of Behavioural Development* 35 (2): 144–51.

Salmivalli, C. 1999. "Participant Role Approach to School Bullying: Implications for Interventions." *Journal of Adolescence* 22 (4): 453–59.

Sbarbaro, V., & T.M.E. Smith. 2011. "An Exploratory Study of Bullying and Cyberbullying Behaviors among Economically/Educationally Disadvantaged Middle School Students." *American Journal of Health Studies* 26 (3): 139–51.

Scheithauer, H., T. Hayer, F. Petermann, & G. Jugert. 2006. "Physical, Verbal, and Relational Forms of Bullying among German Students: Age Trends, Gender Differences, and Correlates." *Aggressive Behavior* 32 (3): 261–75.

Schneider, S.K., L. O'Donnell, A. Stueve, & R. Coulter. 2012. "Cyberbullying, School Bullying, and Psychological Distress: A Regional Census of High School Students." *American Journal of Public Health* 102 (1): 171–77.

Schonert-Reichl, K.A., V. Smith, A. Zaidman-Zait, & C. Hertzman. 2012. "Promoting Children's Prosocial Behaviors in School: Impact of the 'Roots of Empathy' Program on the Social and Emotional Competence of School-Aged Children." *School Mental Health* 4: 1–21.

Schrader, A., & K. Wells. 2005. "Queer Perspectives on Social Responsibility in Canadian Schools and Libraries: Analysis and Resources." *School Libraries in Canada* 24 (4). Accessed 22 May 2006. www.researchgate.net/publication/240622933_Queer_ Perspectives_on_Social_Responsibility_in_Canadian_Schools_and_Libraries_Analysis _and_Resources.

Schwartz, D., A.H. Gorman, J. Nakamoto, & T. McKay. 2006. "Popularity, Social Acceptance, and Aggression in Adolescent Peer Groups: Links with Academic Performance and School Attendance." *Developmental Psychology* 42 (6): 1116–27.

Shariff, S., & D.L. Hoff. 2007. "Cyberbullying: Clarifying Legal Boundaries for School Supervision in Cyberspace." *International Journal of Cyber Criminology* 1 (1): 76–188.

Siann, G., M. Callaghan, P. Glissov, R. Lockhart, & L. Rawson. 1994. "Who Gets Bullied? The Effect of School, Gender and Ethnic Group." *Educational Research* 36: 123–34.

Siann, G., M. Callaghan, R. Lockhart, & L. Rawson. 1993. "Bullying: Teachers' Views and School Effects." *Educational Studies* 19 (3): 307–21.

Singer, E. 2005. "The Strategies Adopted by Dutch Children with Dyslexia to Maintain their Self-Esteem when Teased at School." *Journal of Learning Disabilities* 38: 441–23.

Sittner Hartshorn, K.J., L.B. Whitbeck, & D.R. Hoyt. 2012. "Exploring the Relationships of Perceived Discrimination, Anger, and Aggression among North American Indigenous Adolescents." *Society and Mental Health* 2 (1): 53–67.

Skinner, J.A., & R.M. Kowalski. 2013. "Profiles of Sibling Bullying." *Journal of Interpersonal Violence* 28 (8): 1726–36.

Slee, P.T. 1995. "Peer Victimization and its Relationship to Depression among Australian Primary School Students." *Personality and Individual Differences* 18 (1): 57–62.

Slonje, R., & P.K. Smith. 2008. "Cyberbullying: Another Main Type of Bullying?" *Scandinavian Journal of Psychology* 49: 147–54.

Smith, J.D., J.B. Cousins, & R. Stewart. 2005. "Anti-bullying Interventions in Schools: Ingredients of Effective Programs." *Canadian Journal of Education* 28 (4): 739–62.

Smith, J.D., B.H. Schneider, P.K. Smith, & K. Ananiadou. 2004. "The Effectiveness of Whole-School Antibullying Programs: A Synthesis of Evaluation Research." *School Psychology Review* 33 (4): 547–60.

Smith, P.K. 2012. "Cyberbullying and Cyber Aggression." In *Handbook of School Violence and School Safety: International Research and Practice*, edited by S.R. Jimerson, A.B. Nickerson, M.J. Mayer, & M.J. Furlong, 93–103. New York, NY: Routledge.

Smith, P.K., & P. Brain. 2000. "Bullying in Schools: Lessons from Two Decades of Research." *Aggressive Behavior* 26: 1–9.

Smith, P.K., H. Cowie, R.F. Olafsson, A.P.D. Liefooghe, A. Almeida, H. Araki, et al. 2002. "Definitions of Bullying: A Comparison of Terms Used, and Age and Gender Differences in a Fourteen-Country International Comparison." *Child Development* 73 (4): 1119–33.

Smith, P.K., C. del Barrio, & R. Tokunaga. 2013. "Definitions of Bullying and Cyber Bullying: How Useful Are the Terms?" In *Principles of Cyberbullying Research: Definition, Methods, and Measures*, edited by S. Bauman, J. Walker, & D. Cross, 26–45. New York & London: Routledge.

Smith, P.K., C. Salmivalli, & H. Cowie. 2012. "Effectiveness of School-Based Programs to Reduce Bullying: A Commentary." *Journal of Experimental Criminology* 8: 433–41.

Solomon, S. 2004. "Kids Say the Funniest Things... Anti-homophobia Group Work in the Classroom." *Teaching Education* 15 (1): 103–6.

Solomon, S. & V. Russel. 2004. "Addressing Homophobic Bullying in the Elementary Classroom." *Orbit* 34 (2): 24.

"Star Wars Kid Settles Lawsuit." 2006. *The Gazette*, 8 April. Accessed 2 February 2014. www.canada.com/globaltv/quebec/news/story.html?id=e93a2a11-11c9-4d97 -82ed-221d6cfa1ef2&k=14313.

Statistics Canada. 2007. *Participation and Activity Limitation Survey 2006: Tables*. Ottawa: Statistics Canada.

———. 2012. *2011 Census of Population: Families, Households, Marital Status, Structural Type of Dwelling, Collectives. The Daily, Wednesday, September 19, 2012*. Ottawa: Statistics Canada.

————. 2013. *2011 National Household Survey: Immigration, Place of Birth, Citizenship, Ethnic Origin, Visible Minorities, Language and Religion. The Daily, Wednesday, May 8, 2013.* Ottawa: Statistics Canada.

Stauffacher, K., & G.B. DeHart. 2006. "Crossing Social Contexts: Relational Aggression between Siblings and Friends during Early and Middle Childhood." *Journal of Applied Developmental Psychology* 27 (3): 228–40.

Stein, N. 1995. "Sexual Harassment in School: The Public Performance of Gendered Violence." *Harvard Educational Review* 65 (2): 145–62.

————. 1999. "Gender Violence in Elementary and Secondary Schools." *Women's Studies Quarterly* 27 (42): 212–17.

————. 2003. "Bullying or Sexual Harassment? The Missing Discourse of Rights in an Era of Zero Tolerance." *Arizona Law Review* 45 (3): 787–99.

Stein, J.A., R.L. Dukes, & J.I. Warren. 2007. "Adolescent Male Bullies, Victims, and Bully-Victims: A Comparison of Psychosocial and Behavioural Characteristics." *Journal of Pediatric Psychology* 32 (3): 273–82.

Stevens, V., P. Van Oost, & I. De Bourdeaudhuij. 2000. "The Effects of an Anti-bullying Intervention Programme on Peers' Attitudes and Behaviour." *Journal of Adolescence* 23 (1): 21–34.

Stone, M., & S. Couch. 2002. "Teachers' Attitudes toward Sexual Harassment and Perceptions of Student Peer Sexual Harassment." *Journal of Family and Consumer Sciences Education* 20 (2): 46.

Strom, P., & R. Strom. 2012. "Growing up with Social Networks and Online Communities." *The Education Digest* 78 (1): 48–51.

Strom, P., R. Strom, C. Wing, & T. Beckert. 2009. "Adolescent Learning and the Internet: Implications for School Leadership and Student Engagement in Learning." *NASSP Bulletin* 93 (2): 111–21.

Sullivan, H.S. 1953. *The Interpersonal Theory of Psychiatry.* New York: Horton.

Suniti Bhat, C. 2008. "Cyber Bullying: Overview and Strategies for School Counsellors, Guidance Officers, and All School Personnel." *Australian Journal of Guidance & Counselling* 18 (1): 53–66.

Taylor, C., & T. Peter. 2011. "'We Are Not Aliens, We're People, and We Have Rights.' Canadian Human Rights Discourse and High School Climate for LGBTQ Students." *Canadian Review of Sociology* 48 (3): 275–312.

Taylor, C., T. Peter, T.L. McMinn, T. Elliott, S. Beldom, A. Ferry, et al. 2011. *Every Class in Every School: The First National Climate Survey on Homophobia, Biphobia, and Transphobia in Canadian Schools: Final Report.* Toronto, ON: Egale Canada Human Rights Trust.

Telljohann, S.K., & J.H. Price. 1993. "A Qualitative Examination of Adolescent Homosexuals' Life Experience: Ramifications for Secondary School Personnel." *Journal of Homosexuality* 26 (1): 41–56.

Thompson, D., I. Whitney, & I. Smith. 1994. "Bullying of Children with Special Needs in Mainstream Schools." *Support for Learning* 9 (3): 103–6.

Thurlow, C. 2001. "Naming the 'Outsider Within': Homophobic Pejoratives and the Verbal Abuse of Lesbian, Gay and Bisexual High-School Pupils." *Journal of Adolescence* 24 (1): 25–38.

Timmerman, G. 2003. "Sexual Harassment of Adolescents Perpetrated by Teachers and by Peers: An Exploration of the Dynamics of Power, Culture, and Gender in Secondary Schools." *Sex Roles* 48: 231–44.

Townsend-Wiggins, C. 2001. *Teachers' Perceptions of and Interventions in Episodes of*

Bullying in Schools. PhD diss., Louisiana Tech University. ProQuest, UMI Dissertations Publishing.

Ttofi, M.M., & D.P. Farrington. 2009. "What Works in Preventing Bullying: Effective Elements of Anti-bullying Programs." *Journal of Aggression, Conflict, and Peace Research* 1 (1): 13–24.

———. 2011. "Effectiveness of School-Based Programs to Reduce Bullying: A Systematic and Meta-analytic Review." *Journal of Experimental Criminology* 7 (1): 27–56.

———. 2012. "Bullying Prevention Programs: The Importance of Peer Intervention, Disciplinary Methods and Age Variations." *Journal of Experimental Criminology* 8: 443–62.

Ttofi, M.M., D.P. Farrington, F. Losel, & R. Loeber. 2011a. "The Predictive Efficiency of School Bullying versus Later Offending: A Systematic/Meta-analytic Review of Longitudinal Studies." *Criminal Behaviour and Mental Health* 21: 80–89.

———. 2011b. "Do the Victims of School Bullies Tend to Become Depressed Later in Life? A Systematic Review and Meta-analysis of Longitudinal Studies." *Journal of Aggression, Conflict, and Peace Research* 3 (2): 63–73.

Tucker, C.J., D. Finkelhor, H. Turner, & A. Shattuck. 2013. "Association of Sibling Aggression with Child and Adolescent Mental Health." *Pediatrics* 132 (1): 79–84.

Tutty, L.M. 2002. *School-Based Violence Prevention Programs: A Resource Manual to Prevent Violence against Girls and Young Women.* Accessed 29 October 2008. www.ucalgary.ca/resolve/violenceprevention/English/pdf/RESOURCEMANUAL.pdf.

Tutty, L., & C. Bradshaw, W.E. Thurston, A. Barlow, P. Marshall, L. Tunstall, et al. 2005. *School Based Violence Prevention Programs: Preventing Violence against Children and Youth,* rev. ed. Calgary, AB: RESOLVE Alberta. www.academia.edu/1597984/School_based_violence_prevention_programs_Preventing_violence_against_children_and_Youth_Revised_Ed.

Underwood, M.K., B.R. Galen, & J.A. Paquette. 2001. "Top Ten Challenges for Understanding Gender and Aggression." *Social Development* 10: 248–66.

Underwood, M.K., L.H. Rosen, D. More, S. Ehrenreich, & J.K. Gentsch. 2012. "The BlackBerry Project: Capturing the Content of Adolescents' Electronic Communication." *Developmental Psychology* 48: 295–302.

UNICEF. 2007. *Child Poverty in Perspective: An Overview of Child Well-Being in Rich Countries,* Innocenti Report Card 7. Florence, Italy: UNICEF, Innocenti Research Centre.

———. 2013a. *Child Well-Being in Rich Countries: A Comparative Overview,* Innocenti Report Card 11. Florence, Italy: UNICEF Office of Research.

———. 2013b. *Convention on the Rights of the Child.* Accessed 5 February 2014. www.unicef.org/crc/.

Updegraff, K.A., S.M. Thayer, S.D. Whiteman, D. Denning, S.M. McHale, et al. 2005. "Relational Aggression in Adolescents' Sibling Relationships: Links to Sibling and Parent-Adolescent Relationship Quality." *Family Relations* 54: 373–85.

Urban Aboriginal Peoples Study. 2013. "Key Findings." Accessed 3 March 2014. www.uaps.ca/knowledge/key-findings/.

Vaillancourt, T., H. Brittain, L. Bennett, S. Arnocky, P. McDougall, S. Hymel, et al. 2010. "Places to Avoid: Population-Based Study of Student Reports of Unsafe and High Bullying Areas at School." *Canadian Journal of School Psychology* 25 (1): 40–54.

Vaillancourt, T., P. McDougall, S. Hymel, A. Krygsman, J. Miller, K. Stiver, et al. 2008. "Bullying: Are Researchers and Children/Youth Talking about the Same Thing?" *International Journal of Behavioral Development* 32 (6): 486–95.

Valcke, M., S. Bonte, B. De Wever, & I. Rots. 2010. "Internet Parenting Styles and the Impact on Internet Use of Primary School Children." *Computers & Education* 55: 454–64.

Valkenburg, P.M., & J. Peter. 2007a. "Online Communication and Adolescent Well-Being: Testing the Stimulation versus the Displacement Hypothesis." *Journal of Computer-Mediated Communication* 12 (4): 1169–82.

———. 2007b. "Preadolescents' and Adolescents' Online Communication and their Closeness to Friends." *Developmental Psychology* 43 (2): 267–77.

Vreeman, R.C., & A.E. Carroll. 2007. "A Systematic Review of School-Based Interventions to Prevent Bullying." *Archives of Pediatrics & Adolescent Medicine* 161 (1): 78–88.

Vygotsky, L.S. 1986. *Thought and Language.* Translated by A. Kozulin. Cambridge, MA: MIT Press.

Wade, A., & T. Beran. 2011. "Cyberbullying: The New Era of Bullying." *Canadian Journal of School Psychology* 26 (1): 44–61.

Walker, J. 2012. "A 'Toolbox' of Cyberbullying Prevention Initiatives." In *Cyber Bullying Prevention and Response: Expert Perspectives,* edited by J.W. Patchin & S. Hinduja, 128–48. New York: Routledge.

Wessler, S.L., & L.L. De Andrade. 2006. "Slurs, Stereotypes, and Student Interventions: Examining the Dynamics, Impact, and Prevention of Harassment in Middle and High School." *Journal of Social Issues* 62 (3): 511–32.

Whitney, I., P.K. Smith, & D. Thompson. 1994. "Bullying and Children with Special Educational Needs." In *School Bullying: Insights and Perspectives,* edited by P.K. Smith & S. Sharp, 213–40. London: Routledge.

Whitted, K.S., & D.R. Dupper. 2005. "Best Practices for Preventing or Reducing Bullying in Schools." *Children & Schools* 27 (3): 167–74.

Willard, N. 2010. *Ensuring Student Cyber Safety.* Written statement submitted to House Education and Labor Subcommittee on Healthy Families and Communities.

Williams, K., M. Chambers, S. Logan, & D. Robinson. 1996. "Association of Common Health Symptoms with Bullying in Primary School Children." *British Medical Journal* 313 (7048): 17.

Williams, T., J. Connolly, D. Pepler, & W. Craig. 2003. "Questioning and Sexual Minority Adolescents: High School Experiences of Bullying, Sexual Harassment and Physical Abuse." *Canadian Journal of Community Mental Health* 22 (2): 47–59.

———. 2005. "Peer Victimization, Social Support, and Psychosocial Adjustment of Sexual Minority Adolescents." *Journal of Youth and Adolescence* 34 (5): 471–82.

Wise, S., & L. Stanley. 1987. *Georgie Porgie: Sexual Harassment in Everyday Life.* London: Pandora Press.

Wolak, J., K.J. Mitchell, & D. Finkelhor. 2003. "Escaping or Connecting? Characteristics of Youth Who Form Close Online Relationships." *Journal of Adolescence* 26 (1): 105–19.

———. 2007. "Does Online Harassment Constitute Bullying? An Exploration of Online Harassment by Known Peers and Online-Only Contacts." *Journal of Adolescent Health* 41: S51–S58.

Ybarra, M.L., M. Diener-West, & P.J. Leaf. 2007. "Examining the Overlap in Internet-Harassment and School Bullying: Implications for School Intervention." *Journal of Adolescent Health* 41 (6): 42–50.

Ybarra, M.L., & K.J. Mitchell. 2004. "Online Aggressor/Targets, Aggressors, and Targets: A Comparison of Associated Youth Characteristics." *Journal of Child Psychology and Psychiatry* 45 (7): 1308–16.

Young, K. n.d. "MySpace, Internet Predators, and Child Online Safety." Centre for Internet Addiction Recovery. Accessed 14 May 2013. www.icsao.org/fileadmin/Divers_papiers/KYoung-internetadolescense5.pdf.

Yude, C., R. Goodman, & H. McConachie. 1998. "Peer Problems of Children with Hemiplegia." *Journal of Child Psychology and Psychiatry* 39 (4): 533–41.

Index